YO-BXI-621

Winning Is Everything

Losing Is Nothing

WINNING IS EVERYTHING

LOSING IS NOTHING

Elvin Feltner

CHELSEA HOUSE
New York   London
1980

Editor: Mary Shea Tucker

Printed and bound in the United States of America

LC: 80-68579
ISBN: 0-87754-066-7

Chelsea House Publishers
Harold Steinberg, Chairman & Publisher
Andrew E. Norman, President
Susan Lusk, Vice President
A Division of Chelsea House Educational Communications, Inc.
133 Christopher Street, New York 10014

Contents

INTRODUCTION

When I tell people, whether at a business meeting or a social occasion, about my belief that "winning is everything," I get two basic reactions. Some, hearing this statement for the first time, think I am being facetious and treat it as a joke; some think I am advocating a rather ruthless, callous philosophy of winning at all costs (including, presumably, at others' expense or through dishonest means), and they try to talk me out of it.

Both groups are wrong. I am completely serious; but on the other hand, I do not preach or practice unscrupulous methods of achieving success. We all know the adage "It's nice to be important, but it's more important to be nice," and I agree one hundred percent. What I really mean is that winning, be it a game of checkers or the game of life, is the only thing that is worth a damn; it is the only thing to think about, to set your sights on, to make a habit of, to gauge your progress by.

Of course you will not win all the time, and probably not even most of the time. But don't dwell on the losses. That way lies brooding, despair, and the pernicious seed of gradual self-destruction (what I call "negative energy," about which more anon). Concentrate instead on using each loss to assure a win next time—learn from it, improve your style, apply it as a stimulant. You will find that when you win—and if you apply the principles set forth herein, you *will* win—all the losses are wiped out as if by magic. No one remembers them or remembers you by them; you are known by your successes.

There is a book on the market titled *How to Beat Bobby Fischer*, which contains all the chess games Fischer lost prior to winning the world chess championship in 1972. The author and the publisher evidently expected the book to sell because it would shock the public, and they were right: it sold well and even went into a pocket edition.

Now, it would clearly be absurd to think that any chess player could rise to the top without losing hundreds of games. So why would millions of people buy a book that demonstrated such an obvious point? Because *after* Fischer had captured the championship, he was a winner, and all memory of his losses had vanished from the collective public mind. The book caught people off guard, surprised and intrigued them.

A winner wins—that is his way, and it is the only thing that counts, the only thing anyone cares about. It *is* everything.

This tendency to retain only winners in our minds is universal and applies to virtually every facet of life. Just try to think of all the presidents who have held office during your own lifetime. Got them? Now try to recollect who ran against them! Unless you are an above-average political buff, you will almost certainly fail. You may recall, for example, that Dewey ran against Truman in 1948—but what brings this readily to mind is the famous picture of Truman, newly elected, holding up a newspaper with the huge headline "DEWEY DEFEATS TRUMAN," which some overeager editor had prematurely approved. Even a false report of victory is much easier to retain than any other information about the man who did not win!

I do not propose to philosophize about whether our success-oriented social structure is good, bad, or indifferent for each of us individually or for the nation as a whole. There is a place for such reflections, but not in this book. Here I am only concerned with one undeniable fact: that is the way things are. My point is simple: *We remember winners—and only winners; one win can wipe out all the losses that preceded it.*

Winners are liked, imitated, admired, worshiped. *We love winners.* In other words, the bottom line is:

WINNING IS EVERYTHING!

I

THE WINNING ATTITUDE

1. Winning as a way of life

I like winning. This is probably no surprise to you, because you like it too. And so does everyone else.

Yet so few people seem to be habitual winners—the ones everyone admires, the ones who have everything going their way, the superstars, the tycoons, the successes. Far too many people—capable, good, hardworking people—remain in the gray army of the plodders, stuck in a rut of one kind or another. They would like to win, but meanwhile they drag themselves through drab everyday routines, hoping for a ray of sunshine to fall into their lives. This pattern calls to mind the young maiden who waits for the prince on a white charger to come and take her away from it all. The prince doesn't even know she's alive.

In order to win, you must first of all have a *goal*; a *desire* to attain that goal, enough *motivation* to keep you reaching for it, and a reasonable amount of *ability* in the field you have chosen. Then there must be a steady, determined *application* of that ability toward realization of the goal—and if you can come up with a good deal of *luck* besides, it certainly won't hurt.

Luck, that seemingly most fickle ingredient, usually turns out to be an old reliable if you have taken all the other steps. The Latin proverb *Fortes fortuna iuvat*—which can be roughly translated, "Fortune favors the favorites"—contains deep wisdom. It does not really mean, of course, that the laws of chance can be repealed, just that habitual winners are more apt to recognize lucky breaks for what they are and seize the opportunity.

How can you become a habitual winner? Set a high but attainable goal for yourself and exert every effort to reach it. Once you

win, you will experience a warm glow of satisfaction that sur-
passes any artificial high produced by drugs or alcohol. However,
like them, it will also become addictive. You will want to experience it
again; chances are you will set another goal, perhaps in a different
area, and before long, you will make winning a personal habit and
a part of your lifestyle. As Emerson put it, the world makes a way
for the person who knows where he is going.

   *Nothing is more fulfilling and rewarding than winning as a way of
life.*

2. Your first victory

As I said before, winning is a habit among those who always seem to have everything going their way. As with all habits, the earlier you establish the pattern the better. Your wins need not all be in the same area; in fact, they shouldn't be. If your only goal is to make money, you will be a very lopsided person even if all your attempts succeed.

Most winners got the first taste of victory in a field quite different from their eventual careers, but it was vitally important just the same. It showed them what they could do and gave them the confidence to strike out in new directions. Many habitual winners first scored important successes in college sports, in scholastic areas like spelling bees or science projects, or perhaps by making a speech or winning a scholarship.

Take the case of Georges Painvin. In the spring of 1918, near the end of World War I, the worn-out, ragged French army was barely managing to hold the line against the German forces while waiting for American reinforcements. The Germans also knew that the Americans were coming, and they were sure to try a last mighty offensive before the fresh troops arrived. But where would the Kaiser attack? The French could not possibly cover the whole front, and if the Germans concentrated their efforts in one sector they might get through and take Paris before the defenders could stop them.

At this point, the French captured a coded radio message from German headquarters to the front-line command. Certain that it contained the location of the main attack, they gave it to their best cryptographers. They were in for a rude shock: the message was in a new, seemingly unbreakable code. Georges Painvin, a young man assigned to the unit fresh out of school, realized that the future of his country was at stake, and he determined he would break the code if it took him all night.

It took more than that. He went forty-eight hours without any sleep at all, then took a short nap and hammered away at the impenetrable code. He lost thirty-three pounds in less than a week—but he finally emerged triumphant and gave his commandant the decoded message with the location of the German attack. Thanks to his efforts, several French divisions were shifted to meet the advance, which started only two days later, and they repulsed the last major German offensive of World War I.

After the war, Painvin returned to civilian life with new confidence in his own abilities. Where previously he had had no greater ambition than to work as a clerk somewhere, he now went into business and became a highly successful entrepreneur. He was vice-president of a credit firm, director of a mortgage society, president of a phosphate company, honorary chairman of the Union of Chemical Industries, and eventually president and general director of Ugine, France's largest chemical concern. He also served as president of the Paris Chamber of Commerce. But all these achievements, he later admitted, were just feeble imitations of his first victory, the breaking of the German code. That important first win "left an indelible mark on my spirit, and remains for me one of the brightest and most outstanding memories of my existence," he said.

Of course, not all of us are placed by fortune in such a key position as was Painvin, who knew that the fate of his country depended on his efforts, and his efforts alone. The intense motivation that prompted him to give his all may be missing in many cases. But the most important thing is to remember that it doesn't matter whether your exertions mean anything to the world; what counts is whether they are going to do something for *you.* Painvin might have scored his first victory in a completely obscure field and gone unrecognized by history, but it wouldn't have made any difference provided he let it inspire him to the same brilliant successes he subsequently achieved. His own personal satisfaction, which is the main thing, would still have been the same.

The first big win is important, so go for it with all your might. It will serve as the foundation for your life as a winner.

3. The bottom line

In these pages, I will have a lot to say about the bottom line. It is the most essential ingredient of everything we do: the act, the execution, the performance—the signature on the contract, the delivery of the goods, the payoff. Anyone who is successful in any endeavor knows that a fundamental principle is to cut through all the red tape and assorted garbage and get down to the bottom line.

Fred Allen once said of some of his radio network bosses that they walked through their offices backwards all day so that they would never have to face a decision. Such individuals are the plodders, the procrastinators, the bureaucrats—all losers. The one who cuts through inessentials and manages to get down to the bottom line will be a winner.

It is my desire and intention to get to the bottom line throughout this book. It is, in fact, my main reason for writing. It's no secret that there are hundreds of books on how to succeed in every imaginable way. Having been interested in success from quite an early age, I have read dozens of them, and I've found that they share a common fault: they do not deliver what they promise. Each claims to have the secret—how to make a million, how to win friends, how to do this or that—but if you read carefully you realize that it merely tells how the author did it—often under unique circumstances that cannot be duplicated. Thus, all these how-to books fall short of expectations—they never get down to the bottom line.

Knowing when to throw out all extraneous matters and get down to the bottom line is vital. A salesman realizes that in every presentation there comes a time when he has to stop the prospect's stalling and sew up the deal. If he allows that moment to pass, he may have a very pleasant chat, but he will never make the sale; he will have talked himself right out of it.

In any business meeting where someone makes a bold or unusual proposition, you can generally sense when things come down to the nitty-gritty. This is the time when all the reasonable questions have been answered, all the standard objections met. Now the problem is simple: Do we do it, or don't we? It is at this point that the habitual winner makes up his mind one way or the other and commits himself to a course of action. The loser is the guy who now starts bringing up silly matters or telling anecdotes—his way of conveying the fact that he is unable to make a firm decision. He will never reach the bottom line; instead he will wait for others to take a stand and will then hop on the bandwagon, claiming it was his opinion from the start.

Be a winner—get down to the bottom line!

4. Dissatisfaction and achievement

In order to be a winner, you must learn to achieve results. One of the surest means toward that end is dissatisfaction.

Be dissatisfied with the way things are, and you will want to improve them. Nurture your dissatisfaction, and the desire to make things better for yourself will become so strong that it will push you onward. It was dissatisfaction with having to walk everywhere that made primitive man tame the horse so that he could get places faster and with less effort.

Translate your dissatisfaction into a definite purpose. This will help you to concentrate your energies, apply the right principles, and achieve your goals.

By all means, *be self-indulgent.* Try to get the maximum satisfaction out of life in the shortest possible time. Be unhappy about everything that slows you down or tends to keep you in a rut. Be impatient with your own shortcomings and do your damnedest to get rid of them. Set goals, reach them, then set higher and tougher ones.

Mobilize all your talents; if your task requires talents you don't have, you must either acquire them or get help from people who do have them. Sometimes, if your own talents are inadequate, you can inspire, motivate and lead others to help you achieve your goal. They may have the talents, but they may need you to provide the spark.

Henry Ford, dissatisfied with the way his cars were performing, came up with a definite idea for improvement: the V-8 engine. At the time engineers assured him solemnly that it would never work, but Ford had made up his mind. He goaded, persuaded and cajoled his staff into attempting it; he kept at them, worked alongside them, offered them encouragement and bonuses. In a year or so, the engine had been built, and it revolutionized the auto industry. Thus, although Ford himself did not know how to design a V-8, he knew human nature well enough to get the best out of others. The credit for the improvement is his, regardless of who actually did the work.

During World War II, there was a desperate shortage of ships. Henry Kaiser's shipyards usually took six months or more to build a single vessel. Now he gave them a specific new goal: launch a ship every ten days. Impossible? Seeing that Kaiser believed it could be done and spoke confidently of having promised it to the government, his employees started believing it themselves—and damned if they didn't actually do it! In order to meet the goal, Kaiser's shipyards had to develop a whole new system of ship-building, using prefabricated sections, interchangeable parts and improved scheduling of operations. In its way, Kaiser's innovation changed his industry as radically as the invention of the assembly line had changed all industry many years earlier.

In 1919 Clarence Saunders opened a large store in Memphis. Dissatisfied with the delays that resulted because clerks had to fill each customer's order, he came up with the idea of having the customers themselves take merchandise from shelves, put in into a pushcart and take it to a cashier. Although he never coined a name for it, Saunders thereby invented the supermarket. The system was so revolutionary that he offered it on a franchise basis; by 1922 there were over twelve hundred such supermarkets (called Piggly Wiggly stores at the time) all over the land, and Saunders's method of merchandising had become standard for big stores. Once again, dissatisfaction was the motive force behind a winning idea.

In 1938 an office clerk named Chester F. Carlson became dissatisfied with existing methods of producing copies; at the time the only available copying machines were Mimeograph and Photostat, both very slow. He experimented with a dry process that took him twenty years to perfect; more than twenty companies turned his idea down; but in 1958, when the Haloid Cor-

poration of Rochester introduced the process, it spawned a rev-
olution that made Carlson one of the fifty richest men in the
country. Anyone who had bought Haloid stock in 1947, the year
they acquired Carlson's process, would have seen his money
multiply 180 times in twenty years, and the company change its
name to Xerox Corporation. In that same time, the estimated
number of copies made annually in the United States went from
about twenty million to fourteen billion—a seven-hundredfold increase in just one decade. One dissatisfied man changed the
whole country's office procedures and made himself a multi-
millionaire in the process!

If something displeases you, go right ahead and get steamed
up about it. But don't just gripe—*do something!* You'll be surprised what a little "creative bitching" can do!

It is absolutely incredible what can be accomplished when we
really set our hearts on something. You need only leaf through
the *Guinness Book of World Records* to marvel at the limitless
scope of human achievement. Someone has run the mile in
under four minutes; someone has climbed Mount Everest; someone has walked on the moon. There's no reason why your
achievements or mine cannot be just as amazing. After all, those
awesome records were not set by supermen but by human
beings like us. What they did, we can do—if we try hard enough.

So never let yourself be dissuaded from aiming high by the fact
that no one (or at least no one you know of) has done what you
are trying to do. If it can be done at all, *you might as well be the one
to do it.* Wouldn't it be great if the next entry in the records book
was you?

5. Setting goals

Winning is accomplished by concentrating all your energies in a given direction. In order to do this effectively, you must have a clearly defined target.

My first experience with setting a specific goal and winning came when I was seven and lived in the little town of Hazard, Kentucky. There was an epidemic of spinal meningitis, and I was one of the victims of this extremely painful and dangerous disease. Three times a day the doctor came to the house and extracted excess spinal fluid from my back with an enormous needle. At the time there was nothing better in the way of treatment; the disease was considered incurable. You either survived or you didn't—and the mortality rate was high.

As the days wore on, the suffering became so intense I felt more dead than alive. Finally, half-unconscious, I heard the doctor tell my mother in a low voice that there was no further hope and that I would not make it through the night. Boy, I said to myself, is that doctor dumb! He doesn't think I can hear him. Then it hit me—wait a minute! If he's wrong about my being able to overhear him, he's probably wrong about my chances too. Right then and there I determined not only to live through the night but to beat the illness.

Now, I don't pretend to know just where the natural healing process stops and the will to survive begins. All I know is that suddenly I had a specific goal to shoot for—I had to make it through that long night—and I fought like hell to achieve it. I succeeded, of course, and I had the immense gratification of having "cheated" the doctor. It felt so good that later, when he was telling my parents about the possible deforming aftereffects of meningitis, I immediately decided there wouldn't be any—and I won again. Of the many neighborhood children afflicted during this epidemic, I was the only survivor.

Did I regain health by will power, or would the outcome have been the same even if I had not been so determined? It's impossible to know for sure, but my mental efforts certainly didn't do any harm, and very probably they did at least some good. In any case, the experience enriched me far beyond the immediate result of my "miraculous" recovery. It proved to me that I could affect the course of events if I concentrated on a specific goal. With the naiveté of youth I looked on the whole episode as a game I played with the doctor, my life as the stake—*and I won!* Having thus tasted the heady elixir of success, I wanted more. I gradually developed an enduring passion for matching wits and mental resources with all types of opponents, real and imaginary, and beating them at various "games."

For most people the incentive to win is not so clearly a matter of life and death. However, you can convert many problems into an analogous situation to help galvanize yourself into action. For example, suppose you are unhappy and unfulfilled in your job and see no future in it except years of the same old drudgery. Think of it as some monstrous machinery whose wheels are slowly but surely grinding you down. Determine right then and there to smash those wheels, get out of that rut and rebuild your life. Don't let another day go by. *Act now!*

In setting goals, you must be realistic. A goal that is absurdly high or totally beyond reach will only frustrate you; a goal too easy to attain will not give you a full measure of satisfaction. Assess your normal prospects: Where should you be ten years from now? Suppose that the typical person of your education and ability is expected to make $50,000 a year after ten years on the job. Make it your goal to earn a minimum of $100,000 in five years, and you have something to shoot for.

Set a tough but realistic goal—one that's worth fighting like hell for!

6. Attaining goals

To be a winner, you must be a goal-oriented person. Goals—specific, well-defined goals—are the stepping-stones to success.

Everyone wants to succeed, but very few people are habitual winners. Why? Because success is a nebulous quantity, a relative term. To a bum, success may mean getting a handout from two people in a row; but he is not a winner.

You cannot go after something as ill defined as "success." You must break it down and decide exactly what you mean by it. Will you consider yourself a success if you have a certain income per year? If you become an independent businessman? If you write a book or paint a picture? If you find inner peace and contentment? If you are elected to political office? Is your particular success a Nobel Prize or a Pulitzer? A Ph.D.? A million dollars? It makes little difference whether the goal is material, spiritual or a little of both; just make sure it is perfectly clear in your mind.

Once you have a major long-term goal, it will help to subdivide it into a number of smaller, more immediate goals, each being a step that will take you closer to the big one. Thus, you may have to set a goal for today, for this week, for this month; you may set a target date for accomplishing some specific subordinate part of your task, such as earning a required diploma or setting aside the amount needed for a down payment.

For example, assume that becoming a movie magnate is your aim in life. You will never run across a want ad offering such a position: you must find it yourself. There are several channels through which you can pursue your goal; rarely does a career offer but one path to success.

So, assume further that you subdivide your overall goal as follows.

1. Get the required educational background (film and television courses, workshops, a degree in visual communications and media).
2. Write and direct a thirty-minute short subject.
3. On the strength of this, join an existing television production unit.
4. Become an independent television producer.
5. Switch to theatrical film production as soon as possible.

Now you have an outline of what it will probably take to get where you are going. Each step may take a few years; each will be tough and worth fighting for.

As you begin to act, you will find that each step may again be subdivided. For example, Step 2 will take some doing. Will you want to use your own money to finance your film? Or will you be able to do it only if you can get a government grant? In the latter case, you will have a whole new step-by-step list to follow. Perhaps you plan to persuade others to join you in the venture. Again, new goals arise. How will you market the short? Will it be a pilot for a series? A documentary for public television? An experimental artistic project? What is your target audience and your reason for believing that anyone will want to buy the short?

As you define the specifics, your thinking will tend to crystallize. Instead of vaguely visualizing what you'd like to be, you are pinning down how, where, with what means and when you are going to do certain concrete things. "Becoming a movie magnate" is too huge and general a task, but "talking ten others into investing $1,000 apiece in an interesting television short" is a chore you can start working on.

The deeper you get into a subject, the clearer it becomes just what your next step must be. New vistas will open; there may be shortcuts you had never thought of; more likely, there will be new obstacles and intermediate steps you never imagined. In the end, these will simply become new or different goals that can be broken down into specifics and accomplished in a certain number of steps in a given period of time.

The main thing is never to lose sight of your primary objective and never to let anything deflect you from the intermediate steps leading to the objective. Every goal you actually attain will put you closer to acquiring the habit of winning. Every goal you miss will help you recognize your mistakes—you may have set impossible targets, or perhaps you have not concentrated your energies fully; in any case, you must take corrective steps.

As you begin tasting minor victories, you will grow bolder and start setting your sights higher. *Setting goals is an acquired skill— attaining them, a well-deserved thrill.*

7. Changing goals

A word about changing goals. The human mind being what it is, it is perfectly natural that we sometimes decide to alter course. A goal that seemed irresistible when you were fifteen may lose all its attractiveness by the time you reach twenty-five or thirty. If somewhere along the way you find that you are no longer interested in your original objective but want something else more urgently, it is perfectly proper to rearrange your priorities.

However, there are a few basic facts you should bear in mind. Adjusting your sights as you mature is natural and normal and is one of the signs of growth; but flitting from goal to goal after you have reached maturity is a sympton of some problem—emotional insecurity, lack of confidence, unresolved conflicts or other maladjustments. These are all weaknesses that will slow you down and prevent you from applying your energies to the main task, which is to realize your own potential to the fullest.

To be a winner, you must know what you are and where you stand now, and what you want to be and where you want to be in the future. If you're somewhere between twenty-five and thirty-five and still don't have a direction, or worse yet, don't want anything badly enough to make it a lifetime goal, you have a problem to solve before you can think of becoming a winner in the game of life.

If you are inclined to change goals in midstream, analyze your motivation first. Are you making a switch because your original goal has proved too tough and you think the alternative will be easier? That would be admitting failure. If you really still want the original goal but have decided to settle for second best, your self-confidence will be undermined, and getting back on the winning track will be difficult if not impossible. Better in such a case to grit your teeth and keep on trying. But suppose you analyze your situation and find that the original goal is definitely no longer in the picture; you want something else now, and you want it emphatically. Fine! Whenever you want something very badly, the best thing is to go for it.

If you do decide to make a change, it is important to consider how great an upheaval it will cause. Imagine that you have been studying medicine for five years to become an internist, but now you decide to become a psychiatrist instead. Much of your training can be utilized in your new profession, and the switch will be easy if you don't mind a negligible loss of time—one or two years at most.

But if you decide to become a lawyer instead of a doctor, you are faced with throwing out five years of training and starting all over in a fresh direction. Can it be done? Of course it can; I do not doubt for a minute that it has been done many times, and quite successfully too.

The important thing to remember is this: the more radical the change, the more effort you will have to expend, and the longer the odds against success. At this point you must use your discretion; after all, you know yourself best. Have you got the stamina it will take? Are you truly determined—firmly, irrevocably determined—to fight the odds and become a winner despite the handicaps you have saddled yourself with?

If you answer yes, then by all means change horses in midstream, and to the devil with the consequences—just as long as you are certain that your new goal is the real thing.

8. Getting organized

Once you have decided what you want to be and committed yourself to a course of action destined to accomplish your goal, you must become very methodical. A lot of small, intermediate steps have to be taken, and somehow in your scheme of things you must find the time and the means.

It seems to help to write things down—even if only little reminders like the ones we use to pay the gas bill on time or buy another quart of milk. Here's what I used to do: I put down all the things I had to do on three-by-five index cards and pinned them on the back of my office door. Pretty soon I found that the door was virtually covered with cards and looked very messy. Maybe it was the mess that irritated me more than anything else, but at any rate I was quite eager to clear the door. I attacked the tasks one by one, and as each was completed I removed the card, making the door neater and neater as I came nearer my goal. I removed the last card one day as I was leaving the office for good. It said, "Acquire the business and hire your own replacement." And I did just that. I bought the business and installed a new manager in my old office.

I don't pin cards on my door anymore, but I still write myself reminders. And I still subdivide my major goals into steps and cross them off as I go along.

You will have to organize your available time to accommodate the tasks you have set for yourself. Chances are that when you first look at all you must do, you will feel that it's impossible, given your already busy schedule. But don't be a quitter before you even start! Learn to make use of the elasticity and flexibility of time.

What do I mean by this? Haven't you ever noticed that it is the busiest people who always seem to have the time to see you? And why? Because they know how to use time; in an hour they probably do as much work as a plodding bureaucrat completes in a week.

I am always suspicious of people who tell me they cannot see me for the next three weeks because their calendars are full. Either they are deliberately dodging me (in which case, why force myself on them?), or they sincerely believe they cannot spare a few minutes (meaning that they are hopelessly disorganized and I probably wouldn't get anywhere talking to them anyway). People who simply do not seem to have the time are usually better left alone. It may just be a coincidence, but in several instances where I was put off by an extremely busy executive, when I called again a few months later I found that such-and-such was no longer with the company. Probably too busy to do the work.

Let me solemnly assure you that you do have the time. If you want to be a winner, you'd better have it! Organize it, stretch it, use it more effectively—do whatever it takes to conclusively prove to yourself that the time is there.

Organizing yourself may involve getting rid of ingrained habits that slow you down or immobilize you. I'll never forget the time I called a company at 8:59 a.m. and had to wait a full minute until someone answered. When I asked what took so long, the receptionist informed me irritably that her day started at 9:00 a.m. and not a moment before. To me, this is a pathetic case of a born loser, but such attitudes are far more common than you would imagine. There are people who truly believe they cannot possibly make a move until something happens: until they've had their cup of coffee, until the nine o'clock whistle blows. Like Pavlov's dogs, they have learned to salivate when the coffee break comes along, and so on through the day.

Sheer nonsense! True, your body needs the stimulation of food and drink, and you need rest once in a while. But nature has never printed a schedule for you. It's not your body that objects when you choose to start work at 5:00 a.m. instead of 9:00, it's your mind. And your mind can be controlled. Don't be defeated by the tyranny of conditioned reflexes and social rituals.

If you are really sincere about leaving the rut and learning to become a winner, you can and should work anytime and any-place you feel like working. In real life, as opposed to the Kafka-esque world of bureaucracy, your accomplishments are not mea-sured by the hours you put in or the coffee breaks you take, but by results alone. And there is no time limit on results.

Where time is concerned, the bottom line is simple: *You can if you will.* To be a winner, you must be organized so that whatever has to be done can and will be done.

9. Learning how to learn

The more you know, the better off you are. Your chances of becoming a winner increase as your knowledge broadens.

This is not to say that you need a college degree to be a success. Knowledge can be gathered in other ways as well, including life experience and self-education. Many an individual has become a winner without anything but the most rudimentary formal education. Much depends on how well you apply what you know. There are many stories of college graduates who end up flunking the most demanding course of all—Life. So degrees and diplomas alone are obviously not the answer, or at least not the total answer.

Education is absolutely essential; formal education is simply the best and most convenient way to acquire it. But you must know what you are doing and why before education will do you any good. That's why the most important ingredient of any educational course is *understanding*. If you use schools only to pick up a few facts and learn to perform certain minimal functions, you're not getting an education, you're just being trained. And as you know, dogs, chimpanzees and even fleas can also be trained. But they cannot be educated because it is impossible to add to their training the most precious of all ingredients, understanding. It is that which separates man from beast.

If you leave high school or college with good marks but without an understanding of yourself, of your aim in life and the means of achieving it, you have wasted your time. Worse, you will be joining the great mass of half-educated, half-baked pseudo-intellectuals who somehow manage to breeze through any number of years in school without the slightest inkling of what life is all about—but who, diplomas firmly clutched in hand, are quite certain they know everything.

A little learning is a dangerous thing. Those are among the truest words ever spoken. Much of the world's misery is due to muddleheaded halfwits who latch onto some partly digested theory and arrogantly assume they know enough to run the affairs of mankind. Since they are not genuinely educated and have no real understanding of life, they inevitably fail—but often not until they have inflicted a lot of suffering and damage. There is nothing more frightening than ignorance in action.

The result of education without understanding is a generation of blind adherents to dogmas or slogans. Such people rigidly apply the few scraps they have gleaned to all life's situations, unable to perceive the larger picture.

Liberalism is an example of such a doctrine. Eagerly adopted by the half-educated, it has been turned into a farce. We now have a system of justice that gives all the rights to the criminal and turns the most vicious hoodlums out onto the street to prey upon a helpless society. We are afraid to institutionalize people, and so we have the maladjusted and the insane roaming around loose. We do not like violence, and so we submit to the blackmail of any moronic fringe that uses violence.

Why do these things happen? Because people look to education for magic formulas instead of using it to deepen their understanding of life. The history of the Soviet Union provides a perfect illustration of this point. Lenin, seeing that something is amiss in his native Russia, seeks an explanation and finds one in the writings of Marx. After seizing power, he discovers that people do not behave in accordance with Marx's theory. What does he do? Abandon the idea, like a sensible person? Of course not! Like all the witless semi-intellectuals, he now tries to make life fit the theory. He creates a huge apparatus of coercion so that people will be "forced to be free." And in the end he winds up doing exactly the opposite of what he set out to do. Instead of freeing the workers and abolishing the ruling class, he has created a system of total enslavement, far worse than the mere physical enslavement practiced under the czars. A perfect example of what a few half-absorbed notions can do if they are not tempered with a large dose of understanding. Lenin understood books but not people; he could act but not reason; he saw visions but not the truth. His education shortchanged him: it only gave him half the equipment he needed.

Never make the mistake of seeing in education a magical shortcut, a secret formula for success. Important as it is, education is only a means of rounding out your personality and enlarging your mental capacity. Do not take the first new fact you pick up and think that you now have all the answers. Your degree is no license to run the world; you still have to use the plain old horse sense you were born with to deal with the realities of everyday life.

Wisdom is not measured in years of study or number of credits; it comes not from a university but from understanding. To develop understanding, you must go beyond a mere educational curriculum; you must go to life itself. By all means, get what education you can, but be aware that it will give you only half the answers. If you're diligent enough, it will also teach you how to find the rest of the answers for yourself, by using your own head. At the very least, it's a good starting point on the way to becoming a winner—and that's where it's at, as they say.

10. The will to win

When he was in high school, my brother, who played four different sports, told me one day that he had never known a team that wanted to win as much as that season's basketball squad. I was sports editor of the local paper, and knowing how important the secret ingredient of desire is to winning, especially in sports, I went out on a limb and predicted they would take the state championship that year. To many it seemed a foolish boast. There were some five hundred and fifty teams in Kentucky, and there were three tiers of eliminations before the top sixteen teams met in the state finals. Little Hazard High School had neither the tallest nor the strongest players, and in fact they had ended the season with several losses.

But if a whole team really wants to win, strange things can happen. At the district elimination tournament, in a crucial game with their traditional deadly rivals, Hazard was trailing by five points with only fifteen seconds to go. Every member of the team played like a man possessed—and they managed to get three quick baskets in before the whistle. They survived the next level, the regional eliminations, and then they had to play four games in the state finals. The third game was the killer: Hazard was facing the strongest team in the state. The other team had weight, height and an outstanding record in their favor. The Hazard players knew they had to make every basket count, give it everything they had. To this day, I have the Louisville paper (shades of "Dewey Defeats Truman!") that had gone to press early and had the other team scheduled to play for the championship next day.

But Hazard won that game and went on to win the championship that year—only the second time our little school had won the title. It was clearly the will to win that made the difference.

The Louisville sportswriter, not understanding this, was so puzzled that he thought the result was some kind of mistake. It was no mistake; there was a powerful force at work—a real, sincere, honest desire to win.

Since winning is so integral to sports, it is instructive to watch the teams and individuals at the top. In major league baseball, pro football and so on, the players' abilities are so well matched that for all practical purposes they can be considered equals. Still, some of them win and some lose. Apart from the effect of sheer luck—usually not very great—the difference lies in the "something extra" that some players have. And that is the *urgent motivation to win.*

In each team sport, you can observe the phenomenon of the sparkplug, the one player who seems to motivate and inspire his colleagues—Reggie Jackson, Joe Namath, Pélé. He may not be the best or highest-scoring individual player, but when he shines the whole team shines; he's usually the one who starts the winning rally or the crucial play. In others words, he is a habitual winner. He has the desire, and somehow he is able to communicate it to others.

This intense urge to win occurs in other arenas as well. Among show business people, for example, there are performers who are always "on," whether before an audience of thousands or a single person. These compulsive entertainers are among the biggest names in their profession: Milton Berle, Red Skelton, Carol Channing and many others. President John F. Kennedy was another sparkplug. In 1961 the Russians had a sizable headstart in their space program, having put Sputnik into orbit in 1957. Kennedy was able to communicate to the whole nation his intense desire to surpass them. He set a national goal of putting a man on the moon "by the end of the decade"—and, by George, we did just that!

The *will to win* is perhaps the most intangible but at the same time the most potentially powerful ingredient of winning. There is no limit to what your will can accomplish, because unlike physical stamina and material resources, it is not finite.

Everything else being equal, it is the will to win that wins!

11. Winning behavior

So, you have decided to be a winner! You're convinced you have
the ambition, the drive, the endurance, the determination to succeed. You will let nothing interfere with your plan. All right. But
there is still one major obstacle in your path: you! You may be
your own worst enemy without knowing it.

To be a winner, you must have leadership qualities, and you
must be able to convince others at a glance that you have them.
Your social deportment—the impression you make on your colleagues—will be an important part of your success.

To begin with, eliminate any personal habits that tend to annoy
others or make them underestimate you or even look down on
you. Quit all complaining, bellyaching, whining and otherwise
displaying the attributes of a born loser. *Leaders do not complain
about adversity—they act to overcome it!* Is it raining? Don't gripe,
put on a raincoat. Are you living beyond your means? Don't
frighten your family by showing your own fears; look for ways to
increase your earnings, cut your taxes, trim the budget and enlist
everyone's cooperation. A single positive action is worth a hundred tirades, reproaches, complaints and alibis.

There are some techniques that work with people, others that
don't. If you watch how habitual winners act, you will soon learn
the difference. You then must get rid of your negative traits and
pick up the positive ones to the best of your ability.

For close to three decades, Joe Franklin has been hosting a
television talk show in New York City, the nation's toughest, most
competitive market, so he must be doing *something* right. His
show continues to have good ratings and to be profitable for the

station year after year. He has had the cream of show business as his guests, including stars like Eddie Cantor, Judy Garland, Barbra Streisand, Bing Crosby, Tony Curtis and some ten thousand others.

A real winner—and yet he remains accessible to anyone who wants to see him, always taking the attitude that the next person to come through the door of his office is—at that moment, anyway—the most important person in the world. Even if it's a lowly supplicant or a Broadway has-been looking for a handout, Joe is never fazed; he welcomes each visitor with obvious warmth and sincerity, doing his best to help. As a result, even those who go away empty-handed have nothing but praise for Joe, and *he remains a winner!*

Much of our daily social contact consists of such minor courtesies and amenities, yet in their cumulative effect they may identify one person as a winner and another as a loser. For example, I make it a practice to put people at ease. Whether it is a subordinate running an errand or an important client bringing in a big contract, I always try to have a smile and a handshake ready. I arrive at appointments on time or else call ahead and announce I will be late, even if it is only a matter of minutes. I make a conscious effort not to let small daily annoyances rattle me, at least not so that it would affect the way I treat others.

I never walk out on people or throw them out of my office, regardless of the provocation. If I become convinced there is no chance of establishing useful communication, I simply try to terminate the visit as quickly as protocol allows and then cease to do any further business with them. This saves loads of time that might otherwise be wasted on arguments, recriminations and shouting contests.

When a person is leaving my office, I walk him to the elevator or at least to the outer door. Gestures of this sort may appear insignificant, but I believe they have a function. When I escort someone out of the office, I show by act rather than word that I think enough of him or her to take these few extra steps and to demonstrate the fact in front of everyone present in the outer offices.

In a restaurant, no matter what the occasion, I do not wait for the embarrassing pause after the check is presented—I simply grab it. Admittedly this can run into awesome sums, but I consider it an investment in goodwill and in maintaining a winning attitude. Though I do not advocate a frivolous approach to money, there are times when hoarding pennies will lose you dollars in the long run. Always maintain a sense of proportion. Do not let trivial matters bog you down, spoil your day or make you irritable. Only a small mind is unhinged by small things.

Another name for sense of proportion is sense of humor. If petty problems snap at your heels, if you stumble once in a while on your way to success, laugh it off. Never for one second allow anyone to infer that adversity could possibly discourage you, slow you down or turn you back. Just pick yourself up, brush yourself off and continue as if it didn't matter. And if you adopt this attitude, it won't!

To be a winner, you must act like one.

12. Humor and humility

Humor is a desirable attribute in a winner. Humor is the great equalizer; it is a safety valve and regulator that will prevent an excessive buildup of ego.

You want to be a winner, you have confidence in yourself, you want the best; in other words, you have a fairly well-developed ego. That's fine, but there is always a danger of overdoing it: you turn your campaign to win into a holy crusade; you lose perspective, you become totally self-involved, and before you know it you have become a pompous ass.

If you keep your sense of humor about you, this will never happen. Humor will prevent you from indulging in the luxury of vanity; it will release the hot air from your ego balloon. The words *humor* and *humility* have the same root and are related; humor reduces events to a common denominator, helps you to maintain a sense of proportion, and prevents you from taking yourself too seriously.

You cannot fear or hate someone you can laugh at. Dictators know that, and since they operate largely on fear, they invariably do their best to banish humor. There was nothing funny about Hitler's Nazism, Mussolini's Fascism or Franco's regime in Spain; and no one was allowed to make any jokes about them while they were in power.

Humor, in the present context, is basically the ability to laugh at yourself. Anyone can laugh at a joke or at someone slipping on a banana peel; the question is, can you laugh if the joke is on you, if you are the one who has slipped and fallen down? If you can laugh right along with those who are laughing at you, you have a sense of humor. It is rarer than you may think.

Although almost everyone will assure you they have a sense of humor, most people draw the line at what touches them personally. They cannot laugh about their own mishaps, their families, or their religion, their country and their personal affairs. This attitude is a mistake. If we could freely laugh about all those things, perhaps some of the absurdities of our tangled existence would become clearer and could be brushed away like so many cobwebs.

Many things are serious, but that does not make them sacred. They are subject to doubt and ridicule just like anything else; if they have validity they can stand the heat without sustaining a loss. It's the shaky values that have to be artificially protected by the myth of untouchability. Humor cannot destroy a good thing or harm a good person, but it will spot the phony every time. In fact, good things and good people actually gain in stature when tested in the crucible of humor. Abraham Lincoln, Mark Twain and Winston Churchill would have been great men in any case, but their well-developed senses of humor gave them an extra dimension of greatness.

Humor makes you appreciate subtleties. It lights up an issue and helps you perceive the shades of gray between white and black. Humorless people tend to be crass, boorish and immovably one-sided. Tinhorn tyrants who overthrow governments; fanatic zealots pushing holy causes; terrorists who bomb, hold hostages and kill innocent people; the violent, the perverse and the insane—all are grimly humorless people. They lack the saving grace of humility, and they are unable to see any viewpoint other than their own. If they had the capacity for humor, they might see that there is a crack in every facade, that nothing is so simple and clear as to leave no room for doubt. They might realize that their failure to allow for human imperfection and frailty is a tragic mistake no matter what the issue.

Every winner knows that the road to success is paved with many false starts and failures. That's because the world is imperfect and so are we. Humor helps us not only to recognize this but to bear it with a smile, without becoming incensed. Humor makes it impossible to be carried away by self-importance. It reduces big issues to human terms.

Humor acts like a lubricant. It doesn't do anything by itself, but when the machinery of social communication is running, it oils the gears and prevents breakdowns and blowups. The winner knows that laughter is a precious gift and uses it freely and often, whether the joke is on him or not. It makes the burden lighter and brings people together, at no cost but a slight loss of dignity. And that we can all spare!

The road to winning is long and tough. You might as well enjoy a laugh once in a while before you lose all perspective. *Never lose your sense of humor. The sanity you save may be your own!*

13. Health and disposition

Do you sometimes feel depressed, grouchy, antisocial? Don't worry, everyone does—and of course everyone sometimes feels physically indisposed or ill. But do you, under such circumstances, drag yourself to the office and inflict your misery on everyone around you?

Don't. *Never let anyone see you unless you are in tip-top condition.* If you're not feeling well, you probably won't make any headway with your work anyway. If you're facing important decisions or concluding a deal, your personal condition might influence your judgment adversely. Perhaps more important, anyone you meet that day is likely to walk away with a negative impression of you, and you will have lost the intangible goodwill that is often the crucial catalyst in a business deal.

How do you keep yourself physically and mentally fit? It is not the object of this book to recommend any specific health-care regimen but simply to emphasize the importance of staying in shape. Almost everyone today has a favorite sport or exercise, and that is all very well, but sometimes you simply do not feel up to jogging five miles before work. Besides, keeping in trim should not be a major hardship but rather a part of the daily routine.

You can easily get most of the exercise you need by following a few rules until they become a habit. Simply put a little extra muscular effort into any physical exertion you encounter during the day, and you are in effect exercising. When something drops to the floor, make the act of picking it up an exercise. When you're going upstairs, why not take two at a time? Picking your coat off a rack can be exercise in stretching and arm lifting.

Bicycle to work if you can; walk instead of hailing a cab. If you throw yourself enthusiastically into all your physical activities, however minor, you will soon be radiating energy and good cheer. With very little conscious effort you can walk with a sprightly step that is inspiring to watch.

There was once a young man who studied at the Colorado School of Mines. He was rather short in stature, and both his academic and his athletic achievements were mediocre. He threw himself into all sports with enormous élan but never quite made a crucial save or scored the winning point. However, he did have the ability to inspire his teammates. In time, he abandoned his attempts to become an engineer and went on the stage. There he discovered he was not a particularly talented actor, either. Had he been an average person, he would have lapsed into obscurity, never to be heard of again.

But this young man loved physical action and had unbounded zest for life. When he was supposed to sit down on stage, he would throw a leg over the chair and plop down with a flourish. When he rose from a couch to greet a woman, he would leap over the coffee table first. This did not endear him to directors, but audiences loved it; eventually it prompted D. W. Griffith to offer him a job in the movies.

The young man was Douglas Fairbanks. He reached the top of the heap in a very short time simply by doing everything with extra verve, radiating good humor and happiness, flashing an unabashed grin. With little in his repertory but acrobatic leaps and bounds, he became one of the three top earners in the young film industry. It was the sheer exuberance of his performances that sold him to audiences everywhere in the world. *He was a winner because he adopted a winning attitude and communicated it to those around him.*

14. Initiative and momentum

Winning is about twenty percent ideas, thirty percent talent and fifty percent initiative. Even a fool can have an idea, but it takes brains and effort to put it over.

The idea is your desire to win coupled with your plan of action. The talent is the sum of the ability and experience you apply to the task. But it's initiative that transforms all this into reality. Initiative is the crucial ingredient. You must shake off the inertia you find in yourself and in everyone around you. You must stick to your guns and persist in your chosen path in spite of adversity. You must persuade others to believe in you and stick with you. You must build and sustain momentum.

It's a curious thing, momentum. Once a project has it and you've learned how to keep it rolling, it will ride right over every obstacle to success. But if you let it falter for even a second by allowing some detractor, scoffer or doubting Thomas to make you hesitate, the project is as good as dead.

The words *inertia* and *momentum* are well known from elementary physics. As natural laws, they have universal validity in all human endeavor; you'll never know how hard it is to overcome inertia until you've tried to sell an idea that is somewhat novel or off the beaten path. Whether you're dealing with individuals or giant corporations, officials or politicians, civil servants or businessmen, you will find yourself expending ninety percent of your effort just to get them off their duffs. After that, you can breathe easy.

Having overcome inertia, you now have a very precious commodity called momentum. Don't let it out of your sight for an instant. Sooner or later someone will pop up and say your project is impossible; it can't be done, and there's no use trying. Use what momentum you have to steamroll right over the nonbeliever! Have no mercy and no patience with him.

Sometimes the voice of doubt may come not from the outside but from within yourself. Do not back down or retreat; don't even slow down. Let the doubt become so lost in a beehive of activity that it simply disappears. Never give it the dignity of seriously considering it. *If you never think of failure, you'll find you're not having any failures.*

The human mind is a wonderful thing. Whatever it can conceive it can also realize, provided you do not cloud it with doubt and prevent it from concentrating fully on your goal. Obstacles will arise, of course; that's precisely where you need initiative. There are always alternative ways of accomplishing a task. If one strategy doesn't work, the ordinary person is stopped dead in his tracks, but the person with initiative is already off looking for another solution.

The classic description of initiative is Elbert Hubbard's "Message to Garcia," which became the best-selling pamphlet of all time. It says just about everything there is to say on the subject.

In 1898 Cuba was in a state of civil war, and the United States wanted to assist the insurgents in their struggle for independence from Spain. To coordinate the aid effectively, President McKinley had to communicate with the leader of the rebels, General Garcia, who was holed up somewhere in the mountains of the island, no one knew quite where. There was no way to get to him by mail, telephone or telegraph. McKinley wrote Garcia a note and entrusted its delivery to an army officer named Rowan. Without asking any questions, Rowan took off, somehow found a small boat and made his way to the Cuban coast. He disappeared into the interior and three weeks later emerged, having completed his mission.

When Hubbard wrote his now famous essay about this deed in 1899, he pointed out that, confronted with the same assignment, at least ninety-nine percent of people would have said it was impossible and never even given it serious consideration. Fortunately, Rowan was a goal-oriented man. He knew that a million objections fade away into nothing if you just go ahead and do the thing. He knew that a result was wanted, not explanations and excuses. *He took the message to Garcia.*

This ability to follow through on a project and carry it to completion is rare, and more precious than diamonds. No amount of Hubbard's pamphlets, Horatio Alger stories and other inspirational literature has been able to instill the virtue of initiative in the great majority of people. More people would be winners if they learned how to apply initiative. Once you're a winner, no one asks how much work it took; they are not interested in a long recital of the obstacle course you had to cover to get there. And yet that's the heart of the matter.

To reach a worthwhile goal, you must sometimes use every resource at your command. You must employ strategy and tactics, persistence and doggedness, ingenuity and cunning, rational thinking and your sixth sense, patience and hard work, the brilliance of a genius and the stubbornness of a mule. Don't begrudge this prodigious expenditure of effort; when you win you will be repaid a thousand times over.

If you think of your idea as a driver, and your talents as a car, then *initiative is the fuel. There's no driving without it.*

15. Personal salesmanship

Everything was going along nicely in Paradise, but the nights were a bit dull. There was no place to go, nothing to do—until one day Adam looked at Eve and said, "Let's!" And that's the way it's been ever since. *Nothing really happens until someone sells an idea to someone else.*

To be a winner, you must have the knack of selling a very special product: yourself. You might think that in our society, where the art of selling is so highly developed—just look at the commercial messages that constantly bombard us—everyone would be aware of sales techniques and skilled in practicing them. This is not necessarily so. For example, politics is largely a matter of selling personalities to voters. Yet most politicians wisely do not attempt to do the selling job themselves; they hire publicity people to tell them how best to do it. Even a person who owes all his success to smiles and handshakes obviously needs expert help to sell himself.

Let's assume that you already know the basic requisites of social communication. You know that a pleasant appearance, good manners and a positive attitude will get you farther than grouching. Now you must go beyond that. In order to be a winner, you have to adopt an attitude that will make people want to follow you, support you, buy your ideas and accept your leadership.

One of the fundamental tenets of salesmanship is to believe in your product. If you yourself are absolutely convinced that what you're selling is beneficial and superior in every way, you will be able to make others believe it too. Clearly, then, where the product is yourself, it's self-confidence you need. It must be unshakable, and you must be able to radiate it so that people can see it. You'll never make others believe what you don't believe yourself!

When you're selling your ideas, do it with enthusiasm. It's amazing how enthusiasm can sweep people along and create that precious quality, momentum—that intangible force that gets the ball rolling and keeps it going. When you are intent on making a sale or proposing a course of action that requires others to support you, do not be distracted by scoffers, doubters and arguers. Counter their objections with a courteous acknowledgment, but do not be sidetracked into irrelevant issues that dissipate the impact of your enthusiasm.

A staple of training courses for salesmen is the old story of how to sell a house. When the husband objects, "We can't affort it," the salesman turns to the wife and asks, "Do you think blue would look best in the living room?" Soon he has the couple selecting drapes and has successfully disposed of the issue of whether to buy the house.

There is a good lesson in this example. Often people raise objections to a new project or idea out of fear and doubt, not because they don't believe in it. They are afraid to commit themselves, so they raise issues like "We can't afford it," which of course is unanswerable. Affordability is a purely subjective notion, and a salesman foolish enough to let himself be drawn in by it would soon talk himself right out of his sale.

This same principle applies universally. When you ask people to support you in something different or daring, you will find them raising all kinds of objections as a subconscious defense against committing themselves. Many of their objections are more a test of your faith than anything else; your critics want additional reassurance. So don't be stingy—give it to them. Stress the benefits, the positive side of your idea. If you get rattled and allow yourself to be put on the defensive, people will assume you lack confidence, and you will lose the argument no matter how logical and rational you are.

Two brothers ran a theater together. It seated six hundred people, and on the first night three hundred attended. One brother went to look at the house and came back wringing his hands: "We're ruined, the house is half empty!" The other brother went to take a look for himself and came back all smiles: "What are you talking about? We've got it made. The house is half full!" The second brother was an optimist. He was exercising the power of positive thinking and looking on the bright side. Always seize the positive side of any issue and stress it.

Note how the professionals use this technique. Instead of telling you how much an item costs (the bad news), the ads tell you how much you're saving (the good news). Though just about everyone knows that the alleged savings are often wholly fictitious (because the "full price" against which they are compared was never meant to be charged anyway), people still flock to such sales.

I know a grocer who, whenever a customer picks up an apple, says, "Why don't you take five for a dollar? Otherwise I'd have to charge you twenty cents for that one." Needless to say, nine out of ten buyers immediately grab four more apples and think they've got a real bargain. But what about the customers who see through this transparent scheme? Why, they enjoy a laugh and the good feeling that comes from having proved themselves too smart to be taken in. And that's just what the grocer wants. They are sharing an inside joke with him, and that gives them confidence. They hang around more and occasionally try to see if they can put one over on him and pick up a bargain. The result, of course, is that they spend more money in his store. The man has instinctively discovered the secret of selling himself as part and parcel of the business transaction. People go to the store not just for the merchandise but also for the personality of the owner.

This phenomenon is very common in business dealings. If you can make others aware of you as a person, if you can impress them without frightening them, you're way ahead of the competition. I say "without frightening them" because most people are afraid of anyone who seems intellectually superior. The truly brilliant person, therefore, never shows it and instead tries to put others at their ease. If you have brains, by all means use them—

but use them constructively to solve problems, never to dazzle people. There is such a thing as being too clever for your own good!

Another good way to sell yourself to others is to bring out their best traits. In all dealings with people, it pays to find something praiseworthy about them and let them know it. Make sure your praise is real; if it's something you made up but don't believe, you can't possibly sound sincere. Everyone has qualities that are genuinely worth appreciating, if only we take the trouble to find them. Few of us ever do, and if you're one of the exceptions, you will be noted and remembered. You will have shown that you are really interested in your client as a person, that you are observant and considerate. That always leaves a favorable impression.

More than that, praise often makes the recipient want to live up to the reputation. If you admire someone for his generosity, he will not want to haggle over a trifling sum in front of you. If you praise his foresight and courage, he will be loath to act timidly. Your praise and appreciation, provided they're sincere, may actually help other people realize their full potential. If you say something positive about them, they will want to prove you right. In doing so, they will be helping themselves. And you can chalk up another convert to your cause.

If you can do a good job of selling yourself, you are on your way to becoming a leader—someone who inspires and motivates others, who can evoke their loyalty and support.

16. Perseverance

The great W. C. Fields is said to have observed, "If at first you don't succeed, try again. Then quit. There's no use being a fool about it." Don't you believe it! I'd be willing to bet that Fields himself didn't believe it. He began as a juggler, one of America's best. To be successful at juggling requires exactly the opposite— trying things not once or twice, but hundreds, thousands, tens of thousands of times. Nor can you stop once you have the knack; you must practice for hours every day.

After twenty years as a juggler, Fields switched to comedy and conquered the Broadway stage. Again, it takes enormous discipline to develop a new theatrical craft after years of performing in silence. The art of comedy acting requires a precision of timing and delivery that cannot be mastered after one or two stabs at it.

Some years later, when movies became a major industry, Fields decided to break in. Again he rose quickly to the top ranks. He was already in his fifties, and he made it the hard way, by leaving the cozy security of the Broadway stage and moving to Hollywood, where he was just one of thousands of clamoring aspirants. Anyone who thinks that a movie career was easy for him, handicapped as he was by age and by a far from handsome physiognomy, simply doesn't know much about the film industry.

Finally, when radio began to hit its stride, Fields plunged again. Now nearly sixty, he became one of the most popular stars in yet another medium. I think it's safe to assume that the man who publicly said you shouldn't try too hard did not really mean it.

If there is one character trait that is essential in a winner, it is the ability to stick to it and keep coming back. Winning does not come easy. Edison produced a thousand inventions in his lifetime, yet only one, the phonograph, worked more or less as predicted on the first try. All the others took weeks and months of toil; the search for the incandescent lamp required years of trial and error and the combined efforts of a sizable staff. Every writer, even the very best, can tell stories of a constant stream of rejection slips from publishers, until one day persistence paid off. Every major industry—in fact, every important achievement of mankind—owes its existence to people who knew thousands of failures before they tasted the heady draft of victory. But they stuck to their course, and that's how they made it.

To reach the winners' circle, you must make a habit of persisting in spite of the most discouraging adversities. There is only one exception to this rule: you cannot fight nature. If you persist in the face of natural laws, you will not succeed; you are pursuing the impossible dream. Your own common sense should tell you when this is happening.

Persisting in social relations with people who rebuff you will not work. In fact, it may antagonize them even more. But you already know this—everyone knows you cannot make people like or love you. They either do or they don't; persistence has little to do with it. It's human nature you're pitting yourself against, and that's fatal. In the same way, you know you cannot sell people something they don't want. Products and ideas have their time; you can't fight the trend.

In the late 1950s, several major makes of cars that had sold well for years started losing customers and had to be phased out. Among them were De Soto, Hudson and Packard, all cars that appealed to conservative older buyers. But during the period in question, a new trend had appeared on the American scene: the worship of youth. Despite the demographic fact that the relative number of elderly people in the marketplace had actually increased (thanks to advances in medicine), no one wanted the *image* of being old and conservative, so the cars associated with it had to go. The same thing has happened more recently with Chrysler. People want compact cars at the moment, and bucking the trend is extremely risky—as Chrysler almost found out too late.

Persisting against nature, human or otherwise, leads nowhere. If you find yourself encountering natural obstacles, by all means keep trying, but try in a different direction. There is a museum in Italy that is full of perpetual-motion machines, all of them reposing in a state of perfect tranquility. Quite a few of them, not to mention thousands of plans, drawings and patent applications, were devised long after it had been proven that the concept of perpetual motion violates natural laws. Obviously, rebelling against the established order of the universe will get you nowhere, no matter how stubborn you are.

Outside the realm of nature, sticking to your guns is vitally important. If you are trying to accomplish something that is possible, logical and sensible, something from which you expect to benefit without harming anyone else, then try, try again. *And again!*

17. Focusing on your target

One of the major scientific advances of the twentieth century is the laser beam—a ray of light containing no more energy than an ordinary photographic flashbulb, but so concentrated that it can drill about three hundred holes in the head of a pin. This intense beam can also be used to perform delicate surgery, send signals to spaceships or slice right through solid steel. But the most amazing thing is that within its extremely narrow parameters, the laser light can be as much as eighty times more powerful than the radiation of the sun. *That's the power of concentration!*

Every child knows how to focus ordinary light with a lens to burn wood or paper, but laser technology has refined this principle by a factor of perhaps one million. If you are intent on becoming a winner, then you must apply the same principle to yourself. You must turn your mind into a laser beam concentrated purely and exclusively on your success.

You don't have to have a supermind to do that. Take my word for it, neither I nor a great majority of the habitual winners in this world started out with anything more than average intelligence. Still, by itself an average mind is not enough. It will probably earn you a fair living but nothing more. The competition is simply too great: there are millions of people just like you, and if you use your average mind only to do average things, there's no way you are going to stand out from the crowd.

What you need is to *multiply your mind power by concentrating.* Let's see if we can pursue the analogy of the laser beam a little further. The inventor of the laser noticed that when light hits a faceted gemstone, it bounces off the polished surfaces in several directions. At the same time, it excites the atoms that make up the gem, and they respond by adding a little flash of their own. This is what gives gems their added brilliance and sparkle.

Suppose you could capture all this sparkle and concentrate it. Well, that's exactly what a laser does. It's a gem, usually a ruby, illuminated by a strong light. To make sure that the sparkle doesn't run off ineffectually in every direction, the ruby is completely coated with a highly reflective silver covering except where the light enters and leaves. When a beam of ordinary light hits the ruby, the silver covering forces it to bounce around within the gem millions of times a second, back and forth, until it finds its way out. Each trip, it reacts with the atoms of the ruby to release more and more photons carrying the imparted light energy. By the time it reaches the extremely narrow release opening, this beam of ordinary light has captured all of the sparkle the gem can produce, and concentrated it in a single direction with enormous force.

As you can see, the same principle can be applied to the human mind. Do not fritter away the considerable power of your brain, or it will be like an ordinary gem, sparkling and pretty but not very useful. Concentrate its thinking energy! Keep it stimulated with ideas, but don't let them scatter in all directions. Focus your thoughts into an intense beam of single purpose, and use it to generate action! A little ingenuity can transform a decorative ornament into a powerful instrument. Using the same technique, you can transform your perfectly ordinary brain into a laser-sharp tool of success.

Winners win because they concentrate their energies on winning!

18. Mental discipline

You have just been asked to concentrate your mind's power on a single object: success. But your mind has plans of its own. It insists on taking up extraneous matters; it wants to be coddled, amused and indulged, and it resists the whip.

What now? Don't be alarmed. Like anything else, your mind needs training. You must develop new traits and shed nonproductive ones. *You must discipline your mind to obey your will.* Whenever you find yourself feeling mentally lazy, comfortable or unreceptive, force yourself back on the track. Give yourself a task and see that you apply your mind to it.

It won't be easy. Our mass culture today is oriented toward the sensual as opposed to the spiritual. More than ninety percent of the stimuli you get from the mass media appeals to the senses rather than to the imagination. Tough as it will be, you simply have to tear yourself away from such opiates and start thinking. How much time do you spend watching television? Too much, I guarantee. No matter how pleasant it is to watch Charlie's Angels jiggle, or Reggie Jackson hit a homer, it will seldom do anything for your mind.

It's not that you have to give up all earthly pleasures to be a winner—not at all. But your mind needs stimulation just as much as your senses, and you are probably shortchanging it. If you force it to work, it will learn discipline. Are you "reading" a comic book? Face it, you're not really reading, you're looking at pictures. Throw it away and pick up a real book or newspaper—the *Wall Street Journal* or *War and Peace.* Do you like movies? When was the last time you saw one that made you really think? How many did you see instead that simply surrounded you with sounds, with special effects, with all kinds of appeals to the senses alone?

The only way to train your mind is by *making it work*. Do not permit it the luxury of idling while all the input goes to your senses. The training process may be rather slow at first, but don't make the mistake of trying to speed it up by miraculous short-cuts. The answer does not lie in mind-bending or allegedly mind-expanding drugs, nor in hypnotism, mesmerism or religious cults. It's there in your mind, as it is now, without any additives.

The "mind-expanding" drugs do not sharpen your mental faculties, regardless of what anyone says. On the contrary, they dull and befuddle it. Heroin gets its name from making you *feel* like a hero when you are actually inadequate and unable to deal with life even on the simplest level; it does not *make* you a hero. Drugs only give you the feeling that you're perceiving things better, not the reality. And it's the real world you'll be facing if you want to be a winner—*very real!*

I would also advise you to stay away from mental gymnastics like Zen, sensitivity training and other fads currently on the market under various guises. While they probably do not inflict any lasting harm, there are two eminently practical objections to them: one, they waste time you could be using far more productively elsewhere; two, they tend to turn you inward, toward abstract reflection ("What is my karma?"), rather than outward, toward the practical application of life skills, which is what it takes to be a winner.

True, most of us need a philosophical basis in life, whether a recognized religion or some other spiritual foundation that gives us a reason to live. But it should only be a guide to the general conduct of affairs, not a full-time preoccupation with eternal riddles. No matter how fascinating it is to speculate about life, *it has no tangible value if you cannot translate it into positive action that will make you a winner.*

Reflect for a minute about the connection between the spiritual and the secular. Which of the world's major faiths have given us the most big winners?

There certainly is a large percentage of major successes

among Jews. Is it the God they believe in, or could it have something to do with the fact that they always stress the best-quality education for their children, instill respect for the professions, and consider the handling of financial matters a skill to be carefully cultivated?

The Puritans succeeded not so much because of their religious tenets but because of the famous Protestant ethic—hard work, the value of thrift, and a disciplined approach to life.

The Catholic faith has extended itself all over the world. At least part of its success can be attributed to its stress on the value of property, the sanctity of the family, and the need for territorial expansion (after all, sending a missionary abroad is just like opening a branch office).

The Eastern religions, despite their numerical superiority, have produced relatively few tycoons in proportion to the enormous populations they represent. This is hardly surprising when you consider that regardless of their specific god or belief system, they generally stress asceticism over material welfare, passive reflection over assertive action, and inward-directed thinking about the soul over outward-oriented contact with the world.

The lesson is simple: *You can either think about life or live it.* To live it, you need a mind that's keen and alert—not stupefied by drugs, not dulled by the unrealistic daydreams of mindless mass culture, not burdened by half-digested philosophical questions it cannot resolve. Free it from all such encumbrances and give yourself a chance.

Once your mind is free of clouds and is forced to tackle real life, it will have nothing to fall back on but common sense. And that's precisely the best thing that can happen. Then all you have to do is train it and hone it and sharpen it and force it to concentrate. You'll be amazed how the cobwebs will clear!

Your mind is the most precious tool in your drive to be a winner. *Make sure it's in proper working order!*

A good practical way to concentrate your mental energy is to aim high in life. If you set your goals so high that they appear all but unreachable at the moment, you are on your way to focusing your mind like a laser beam.

Why? Because when you sit down and analyze ways to reach that impossible-looking goal, you soon realize that you will have to eliminate idle, nonproductive activities. (That's equivalent to coating the sides of the ruby with silver.)

You now have to break the goal down into intermediate, halfway manageable steps. This will require some doing. No doubt you will sometimes find yourself in unknown territory; you will have to improvise, devise ingenious shortcuts, discover new techniques. But even the very process of organizing your plan of action will awaken brain cells you never knew you had. (This is equivalent to the light bouncing back and forth in the ruby, exciting it to sparkle.)

In executing your plan, you may have to do things you have never done before, contact people you have not contacted before, break new ground in every endeavor that will bring your goal closer to reality. You have no idea how the necessity for some original thinking will sharpen your mental faculties! Just as a laser cuts through solid steel, your mind's concentrated energies will be able to cut through to the bottom line every time. In this way, without drugs, occult magic or pseudoscientific mental gymnastics, the simple necessity of pursuing your goal with all the resources at your command will force you to make your mind a precision tool of success.

Concentrate your mental energies, and your reward will be a disciplined mind—the best assurance of sanity, reason and happiness.

19. Decisive, timely action

In the spring of 1941, Nazi Germany looked like a sure winner in the battle for Europe. The Germans had blitzkrieged their way into the Low Countries and France on the western front, and in the east they had secured Poland and Norway as staging areas for the planned Russian campaign. But then Hitler wavered. Instead of invading Russia immediately, he heeded the request of his southern ally, Mussolini, and diverted troops to help the Italians mop up a few strategically insignificant nests of resistance in Albania, Yugoslavia and Greece. This operation took only a couple of months and was completed by April. The marching orders for Russia were issued in June.

The delay proved crucial. As a result of the late start, the German troops reached Leningrad and Moscow just before the onset of the cruel Russian winter. Unable to cope with the weather, they could not penetrate the defenses to take either of these major cities. Thus, instead of a virtually certain Russian surrender that would have enabled Hitler to concentrate his forces in the west and attack Britian before America entered the war, Germany was faced with a Russian counteroffensive. Now there was no hope of mounting an invasion of Britain in 1941; and by the end of the year, the Japanese had bombed Pearl Harbor, the United States had declared war, and Hitler's chance of putting a quick end to all resistance had vanished.

How differently it might have turned out had there been no two-month procrastination in the Balkans. These very words might have been written in German! True, we must be eternally grateful that Hitler made this fatal error. But here we are concerned not with the destiny of nations but with the proven fact that taking the decisive step at the right time can mean all the difference between winning and losing.

While we are on the subject of World War II, consider another powerful illustration of this point: the Yalta conference of February 1945, which shaped the nature of the postwar world. It is an open secret today that President Roosevelt was a very sick man at the time (medical records released in 1977 described him as "comatose" during this crucial bargaining session, and he died of cerebral hemorrhage two months later), so that all the real decisions were made by men of far less vision. Because of the lack of strong American leadership at Yalta our military victory in Europe was hamstrung by so many absurd, humiliating and unworkable Soviet-imposed restrictions that the momentum of history shifted to the East. Consider, for example:

1. An unrealistic boundary line—the Elbe River, which we had already reached, but which the Russian army was still months from attaining—was set up between Allied zones of occupation. Result: Germany divided; Czechoslovakia lost to the East; Berlin and Vienna absurdly split into sectors; Berlin blockade and airlift; the Cold War of petty harrassment and skirmishes; erosion of confidence in Anglo-American leadership all over the world.

2. An absurdly lopsided United Nations, with the Russians gaining extra votes for "countries" (Byelorussia, the Ukraine) that were little more than annexed territories. Result: clear proof to all the world that the West is spineless and that even the most ridiculous points can be won at the conference table. How many events that quickly followed these blunders of ours might not have happened had we taken a decisive stance at Yalta—the loss of China, the Korean War, the fruitless, endless negotiations at Panmunjon, Geneva and elsewhere.

The lesson is clear. Appropriate decisive action at the right moment tips the balance every time! Even a painful decision, properly timed, is always better in the long run than vacillation. By deciding to drop the atomic bomb on Hiroshima, President Truman created many enemies and caused the loss of tens of thousands of lives. But had he postponed the decision and permitted the war to drag on, the losses might have run into millions of lives. Truman didn't procrastinate; he willingly shouldered the responsibility. The blame and the glory, depending which side of the issue you are on, are forever his.

He made a rational decision (the lesser of two evils).

He took decisive, timely action (dropped the bomb).

He produced immediate results (the war ended).

In recent years, the problem of international hoodlums using innocent people as pawns in their lunatic schemes has become a major concern for all of us. But just compare the results of timely action in Entebbe with the prolonged suffering caused by American inaction in the Tehran hostage crisis.

In 1976 Arab terrorists seized an Israeli plane carrying 103 persons and hijacked it to Entebbe airport in Uganda. Instead of playing into the thugs' hands by negotiating with them, the Israeli government dispatched a commando group that staged a daring raid on the well-guarded plane, killing more than a score of the kidnappers and suffering only three casualties. By contrast, the taking of some fifty American hostages by Iranian militants in November 1979 has led to nothing but American humiliation. For months the United States took no action of any kind against the aggressors, instead giving undeserved dignity to the Iranian cause by negotiating seriously with them. When it finally came, the abortive military rescue mission was too little too late. The procrastination and vacillation of the American government has done nothing but serve as an open invitation to acts of violence against innocent people.

The whole world respects spunky little Israel. The Six-Day War on the Sinai; the raid at Entebbe; the miraculous transformation of the inhospitable, arid land into a thriving community—all these things were accomplished against incredible odds by a bold people willing to make timely decisions and back them up with immediate, forceful action. *Those are the habits of winners!* Note that not a single one of the Israeli successes can be traced to a diplomatic maneuver; they were all due to clear-cut action, impeccably timed.

There is no doubt that the timing of an act is an essential element of its eventual failure or success. Take the case of Rosa Parks of Montgomery, Alabama. On December 19, 1955, merely because she was black, she was ordered to give up her seat in the front of a bus and move to the back. Not an earthshaking event at the time, and one that must have happened often before. This time, however, things were different—Rosa Parks refused, and her complaint stirred the nation. There followed a boycott, a legal battle and a growing awareness of discrimination in the United States. Gradually segregation, which had been a feature of American life for more than a century, began to crumble away.

Did Rosa Parks just happen to be at the right place at the right time? *It is one thing to get a lucky break, quite another to recognize it as such and seize it.* The credit here goes to the Reverend Martin Luther King, who had heard complaints like Rosa Parks's all his life. On this occasion, he realized that circumstances were favorable, and he used the opportunity to organize the boycott and direct the subsequent legal fight. Like the habitual winner he was, *he knew when to take a seemingly unimportant break and turn it into a major breakthrough.*

But how did he know? Was he in contact with some cosmic consciousness beyond the ken of other mortals? Not at all. He merely relied on common sense—that elusive quality everyone has but so few use. He simply observed what was going on around him. That's how he knew that desegregation could be advanced by a practical demonstration then and there.

When you come right down to it, the milestones of human progress are all ideas whose time has come. Whether they are political systems like monarchy or democracy, inventions like the automobile or the electric light, or social issues like national health insurance or the metric system, the pattern is the same: for a long time, often centuries, men dream vague dreams about this improvement or that, and suddenly there is a spate of activity from a dozen different sources at virtually the same time, and the thing is done. Its time has come: the collective mind and soul that we call society is ready for it.

The winner is the genius who can recognize a trend before everyone else catches on, and who has the courage of his convictions. When the automobile was invented, many people could see that sooner or later it would replace the horse. Henry Ford didn't wait for later; he acted, thereby helping substantially to accomplish the change. The aerial dogfights of World War I showed anyone who cared to face facts that the future of warfare would be in the air. Yet General Billy Mitchell, the only American who acted on this conviction and tried to build up an independent air force, had to fight like hell to get anything done, even suffering the agonies of a court martial for his pains.

Most people can sense a trend, but they are not confident enough to hop on the bandwagon until someone else has taken hold and made it an everyday reality. To overcome this inertia, to seize a trend and work it for all it's worth before the field is crowded—that is to ride the crest of the wave and be a winner!

There was a right time to introduce the hula hoop and the frisbee. In the sixties there was a musical trend toward rock, and just look what the Beatles did with it! When leisurely dining began to give way to fast snacking, up popped McDonald's. The smart leader does not tell people where to go—*he finds out where they are going anyway, then gets out in front and takes charge.*

20. Giving it all you've got

Jim Busby, an outfielder for the Washington Senators, once crashed into the stadium wall and nearly knocked himself out making a spectacular catch in the top of the ninth inning to retire the opposing side. Only at that point it seemed an empty gesture because his team was losing 15 to 1. But Jim Busby was not thinking about that—he was there to do the best he could, and that's exactly what he did. It would be nice to report that his teammates rallied to make up the deficit, but nothing like that happened; the Senators went down to defeat. Still, many players on both teams must have asked themselves that night, "Am I putting out as much as Jim Busby?"

Speaking of baseball, Ted Turner, owner of the Atlanta Braves, once got into an argument with a player, and they finally settled it by pushing baseballs to home plate with their noses, one man from first base, the other from third. There they were, two grown men on all fours, engaged in a preposterous contest over a trivial matter, but Turner tore into it as if his life depended on it, and he scored a clean win. His nose all skinned and bloody, he ran up to the broadcast booth and shouted, "I won!" Turner wore bandages for weeks, but whenever anyone asked him if it was worth it, he'd say, "I won, didn't I?" Since he was a habitual winner, it never occurred to him that anyone could fail to see the point.

Turner first began to show signs of being a real winner at the age of twenty-four, when he inherited his father's billboard business. It was on the verge of foundering, and everyone advised him to sell it as fast as he could. Instead he set about rebuilding it, managed to turn it around, and made it a profitable enterprise. He then bought a down-and-out local television station that was bringing in $900,000 annually in billings; within a few years, he had the annual revenues up to $16,000,000. By using imaginative merchandising and satellite transmissions, Turner then made his station the base of a mini-network beaming local sports and other programs to any interested cable station. He now has the country's first private superstation!

Turner also became interested in yachting. Being a winner, he wasn't satisfied with merely learning a few basics about sailing; he went straight for the pinnacle, the America's Cup—the most prestigious title in yachting. Sure enough, in 1977 he skippered the Courageous, which won the coveted trophy against Australia. It just goes to show . . .

Once a winner, always a winner!

II

THE OBSTACLE COURSE

1. Negative energy

If you ever want to become a winner, you must first meet the challenge of the self-destructive negative force that is in all of us—*and you must beat it!*

Do you smoke? Then you are probably afraid of ruining your lungs and dying of cancer eventually—and yet you still smoke. Doesn't this prove how powerful negative energy is? In olden times, such phenomena were ascribed to evil spirits or the devil. Now we recognize them as the subconscious desire to destroy yourself or prevent yourself from succeeding in life.

On radio years ago there was a fictional character named Elmer Blurt, the world's worst salesman, who knocked on doors saying, "Nobody's home, I hope, I hope." This pusillanimous posture illustrates perfectly what negative energy does: it gives you a built-in excuse for failure. Many people preface any important venture with the apology "I'll try it, but I'll probably fail." Then, when they do fail, they can come up with an I-told-you-so, and in many cases they actually seem to derive some sort of grim satisfaction from the outcome. It reinforces the conviction that this world is too rotten to let them succeed, and it also confirms the belief that inertia is the best approach; next time they will have an excuse for not even trying.

This self-indulgent cowardice is deadly, and you must learn to recognize it in any disguise and get rid of it at all costs. Anytime you undertake something important, there will be detractors saying you cannot succeed. Don't worry about them—and above all don't join them in your own mind! Don't worry about things that are beyond your control or that may happen far in the future;

they are phantoms and chimeras, imaginary monsters that will only distract you from the task of accomplishing the various goals you have set.

The possibility of failure is by far the most important thing you must learn to ignore. Of course, it is always there, but if you let your mind dwell on it you will subconsciously set your sights for it, and you will fail as surely as if you had planned it that way.

But suppose you do ignore the possibility of failure, never mention it, and fail anyway. It seems that you're in for a rude shock because you have not prepared yourself—and what's more, you have no excuse to fall back on. So what? The shock is good for you. Maybe it will make you angry enough to try harder next time. And as to excuses—*failure is always inexcusable,* no matter how carefully the defeatist has prepared his alibis. Besides, nobody cares. Nothing is more boring than listening to the loser explain why he or she should have won.

There is a story about a poor immigrant who came to the United States and opened a small diner. It prospered so much that he was able to send his son to college. Finally the young man graduated and was ready to come into the business. He studied the operation and at length faced the old man: "Look, father, I learned in college that there's a recession coming, and you simply cannot continue to run the business the way you have. Everywhere businesses are going bankrupt, and here you have a big neon highway sign that's costing us money. You serve huge portions and give free seconds on coffee, and you keep the place open long hours, which increases operating costs. You have to cut out all these luxuries!" So the father, proud of his son's knowledge, dismantled the sign, started serving tiny hamburgers and reduced the hours. Sure enough, business fell off rapidly. How right the boy was, reflected the father. The recession sure is here! And before long he was bankrupt, right on schedule.

Whether the anecdote is true or not is immaterial; the point is that it illustrates how negative energy works. As soon as you start thinking of failure, it becomes a prophecy that is only too speedily fulfilled. You begin *acting* like a loser, and from then on there is no hope for you.

How does a habitual winner treat failure? It hardly breaks his stride. The win-oriented person knows that *the only thing that will wipe out a failure is the next success,* and so he simply regroups his forces, redefines his goals, and goes on as if nothing had happened.

Remember the lesson of Richard Nixon, a habitual winner if ever there was one. In 1952, when he was running for vice-president, it was disclosed that he had accepted money from California businessmen for his office expenses. He went on television with his rebuttal, the famous "Checkers speech," in which he shrewdly used his dog Checkers to gain the viewers' sympathy and win a reprieve. Then, in 1960, John F. Kennedy beat him in the presidential election. Most people would have probably quit politics at this point, but not Nixon. He promptly ran for governor of California in 1962—and failed again.

The verdict seemed clear: the American people did not want Richard Nixon. But did he let it bother him? He was a habitual winner; defeats only spurred him to greater efforts. He ran for the presidency again in 1968, and this time he won. In 1972 he was re-elected to a second term with an unprecedented plurality; only Massachusetts and the District of Columbia went for his opponent.

As we all know, in 1974 Nixon was virtually drummed out of office by an outraged public. Why? How could this proven habitual winner suffer such a devastating blow only a year after his terrific electoral triumph?

If you analyzed the events of Watergate and the subsequent cover-up, you could write a textbook on negative energy. First of all, at the peak of his victory Nixon suddenly began *worrying about his detractors*: the Watergate break-in was a misguided effort to find out what secret ammunition his enemies might have gathered. Nixon also committed sin number two—*worrying about things that were beyond his control,* such as the press and television, for whose benefit he staged an equally ill-advised, elaborate cover-up.

Here we have the case of a man who had always marshaled all his efforts on the side of winning but was now wasting his energy chasing after imaginary foes and nonexistent conspirators. Having thus dropped his winning habits, Nixon promptly became a loser, inevitably and inexorably dragging many people down with him. His own negative, self-destructive tendency could not have been better evidenced than by the totally unnecessary tapes that recorded even his most damaging private conversations. Clearly, the man was *preparing his alibi for failure.*

The advance excuse, worrying about detractors, trying to influence things beyond one's control—three sure signs of the negative force at work, leading to certain failure.

What made Nixon, obviously an experienced hand at the game of winning, suddenly let the negative force take over and destroy him? Such intriguing speculations are better left to psychologists and sociologists. What concerns us here is that:

1. the negative force obviously exists;
2. it manifests itself in easily recognizable behavior;
3. it may strike even a confirmed winner at any time if he is not aware of its symptoms;
4. it dissipates energies into wasteful, unproductive channels;
5. it virtually guarantees defeat in anything its victim wishes to undertake.

The negative force is not to be trifled with. Expunge it mercilessly anytime you are tempted to make alibis for yourself in advance, anytime you feel the world is conspiring against you, anytime you find yourself wanting to call on external forces, earthly or cosmic, to intercede for you.

Losing requires no preparation; any fool can lose. But you must prepare yourself for winning; *put your mind into a winning mold and watch out for signs of the pernicious negative energy at work.*

2. Excessive self-indulgence

One of the most frequent manifestations of negative energy is escapism. It is human nature to build castles in the air, and there's nothing wrong with that in itself. After all, in order to win you must have a goal, and that goal is at first nothing but a castle in the air. The secret of winning is to erect that castle on solid ground so that you can indulge in the luxury of moving in.

However, if success does not come fast or easily, somewhere along the road you will be tempted to move into the castle while it is still up in the clouds. Many people seek shortcuts in the booze bottle, the opium pipe, the heroin needle and various other forms of escapism. In reality, these represent excessive self-indulgence, and another name for that is *failure.*

There are no pauses along the road to success. Any bypass or detour will not only make the trip longer but will also sap your strength and your will to return to the main road and continue climbing up the hard way. The only healthy self-indulgence is victory without compromise—attaining the goal you have set in the real world, not in a pipe dream.

Almost anything done to excess is damaging, whether it's eating, smoking, sleeping around or watching television. Even excessive work can be a sin; the workaholic who lives for nothing but business and never takes time out to enjoy his family or a hobby is deluding himself. Underneath he is usually an insecure person, afraid that his business could get along quite well without him, and therefore pretending just the opposite—that it could not survive without him for a single minute.

No matter what you're striving for, things will sometimes get rough, and there will doubtless be days when everything goes wrong. But whatever happens, ride it out as best you can; never allow yourself the indulgence of turning away from the unpleasant reality to one of the tempting escape routes. If you do, it will very likely be the turning point of your career. *Once you start downhill, you will find everything well greased for the slide.*

In a business where there are partners or a staff, there is a built-in temptation to blame the other guy when things get fouled up. Do not succumb to this temptation; shoulder the responsibility. Better yet, don't worry about who caused the problem; it's more important to discover who can solve it. It demonstrates especially poor judgment to blame subordinates; anyone under you is your responsibility, no matter what happens. A Hawaiian proverb puts it best: "He who keeps putting down his inferiors doesn't have any."

All of us now and then find ourselves in the doldrums, on the losing side of a deal, or in a situation where we have done our best but circumstances beyond our control have deprived us of the rewards. More often than not, such setbacks are immediately joined by others, and suddenly we're on the down side of a cycle.

If this happens to you, ride it out. Do not under any circumstances give up the ship! Keep your faith, and sooner or later the positive force will take charge and you'll be back in business—but only if you don't spend the intervening time in self-pity. Bite the bullet if you must, but stay in there and fight. The positive force is on your side only if you have a positive attitude. Self-pity and cowardice are luxuries you cannot afford. Once you sign up for a winning course, you're in for the duration and you must expect a few lumps along the way.

A hard-earned victory is that much sweeter!

3. Alcohol, nicotine and other killers

If you're going to be a winner, all your physical and mental faculties must be in tip-top shape at all times. Therefore, the rule regarding smoking, drinking and drugs is very simple: Stay away.

If you haven't picked up these habits yet, don't start experimenting with them now. Remember all the hopeless addicts, all the vegetablelike beings languishing in institutions, the drunk drivers who have crippled themselves and often killed others, all the living dead full of cancer. Every one of them started just for the thrill of experiencing something; all of them were sure they could handle it.

The fact is, none of us can handle it. Many things in nature are beyond our power to control, and we acknowledge this. No one is fool enough to let a poisonous snake bite him to see if he can "handle" it; the evidence speaks for itself. But how many millions of lives must be destroyed before we accept the evidence that human beings simply cannot handle habit-forming chemical killers?

If you already smoke, drink or use drugs, my sincere advice to you is: *Quit!* I know what I'm asking. I know it's not simple. But then, I never said that being a winner is a simple project.

As a matter of fact, conquering any one of these evil habits should be the first step in your overall plan to become a winner. The reason is twofold: you will clear your mind and body of substances that slow it down and harm it, and you will learn to concentrate all your efforts on a very difficult task. In your drive to win, you will need both a healthy mind and a healthy body, not a befuddled brain and a decaying physique. The discipline and self-control it takes to drop your habits can be used later for more positive achievements.

Perhaps the hardest thing to overcome when you decide to break one of your addictive habits is the fact that they have become socially acceptable. So many social occasions today seem to virtually require that you drink, smoke, take a little pot and so forth. Learn to be firm in your refusal, and don't yield to the persuasion that is sure to follow. Do not let yourself be dragged into specious arguments as to what is "really" harmful, what has been "conclusively proven," and how there's no big problem because "everybody's doing it." People who use such arguments choose to ignore the abundance of proof that already exists and instead try to rationalize their own downfall.

If you want to be a winner, you must travel your own road most of the time. You have no business following the crowd unless you want to join them in a program of slow self-destruction and condemn yourself to a lifetime of mediocrity. Nicotine, alcohol and drugs sap the body's strength and disorient the brain. Since you cannot hope to be truly successful under such conditions, you must make the task of giving them up for good one of your top priorities.

4. Substitute victories

Recently I visited a friend I had gone to school with. He was teaching political science at a small rural college, but it was obvious he was not very happy there. At school he had had visions of a professorship at Harvard, publishing the definitive work in his field and such, but none of it had materialized for him. At lunch he intimated that he also had some family problems: his wife might be cheating on him, and he felt he was losing control of their two children. Finally we got into his car, and he started driving home. He became animated and began explaining to me how, by taking this back road and that shortcut, we could save five minutes or so. He dwelled on the subject in loving detail and later repeated the same information every time we took a ride.

It was clear that this man was losing the battle of his life but "winning" the battle of the country roads. Only there was nothing to be won, no battle: the roads were there for anyone to use, and there was no contest and no victory worthy of the name. It was a substitute victory and, like all imitations, worthless.

When your major goal seems to be eluding you, it's easy to get sidetracked by trivialities that allow you to claim you are scoring "wins." How many times have you run into somebody who prides himself on some insignificant detail—like having twenty-six freshly sharpened pencils on his desk each morning—that is easy to control and therefore gives him the false conviction that he is achieving something. On the surface, such behavior appears harmless enough, but there is an underlying danger that the minor ritual may slowly become an end in itself. If this guy doesn't get back on the main track, and if other frustrations begin to pile up meanwhile, there'll come a time when he'll blame his failure to obtain a promotion on the fact that he was unable to sharpen all those pencils every morning—owing to the incompetence and treachery of his subordinates, of course. From there it is but a short step to paranoia and the life of a confirmed loser.

The tendency to lose sight of the main objective is practically endemic to any large bureaucracy. Thousands of minor executives consider themselves winners if they succeed in pushing around a given number of reams of paper per day, not knowing or caring whether anything meaningful is actually accomplished as a result. Often they simply compile statistics and reports that are filed away somewhere and forgotten—and that would be useless even if anyone did consult them. Yet many people are willing to accept such phantom victories as the real thing and even to make lifetime careers of them.

That is not the essence of winning. Your purpose is not to play games with life but to play the game of life itself; *that's the only one worth winning.* As I said, you can have many goals—some of them so trivial that they can be won with ease. If you say you'll have your own business by the time you're a certain age, you have a worthwhile goal. But if you say you'll get to the office on time every morning or keep your lawn freshly mowed each week, it's a subterfuge. You may accomplish these "goals," but they will not add anything to your success in life.

Only goals that advance your welfare count. Accept no substitutes.

5. Instant destiny

Most people like to gamble. They buy lottery tickets, they play bingo, they bet on horses and baseball games, they go to Las Vegas or Monte Carlo. Gambling is the impulse to win gone astray, the attempt to achieve a win without having earned it. It gives people a golden opportunity to win instantly.

But, as Damon Runyon put it, "All horse players die broke." Though it is possible to win any game once in a while, the long-term odds are always stacked against you, always rigged to favor the house. There is no harm in occasional gambling, provided you understand that you are spending money, not making an investment; but under no circumstances should you risk money you need on a bet, regardless of the hot tip or urgent hunch you have. The real pro doesn't gamble unless he's sure to win.

A big gambling win is an exhilarating experience, but it is not nearly as satisfying as the thrill of having won by your own efforts. More important, no amount of gambling will help you develop the discipline and expertise you need to become a habitual winner in life situations. As anyone in the gambling world will tell you, probably ninety percent of all winnings go right back into the business, since the "winners" all think they can beat the odds and run up a fortune by betting again. *In the game of life, however, your winnings are permanent and remain with you.*

Since the urge to gamble is nearly universal, I do not intend to advise you not to gamble at all, but you should at least understand the odds and try to tilt the wheel of fortune your way. In any game of pure chance, this is impossible without cheating; therefore, the best course is to gamble in an area where your ability or experience increases the probability of your winning.

There is a story, allegedly true, of the little old lady who invested her savings in a few stocks. She had no business background at all, and her broker was amazed that year after year she made a killing. Finally he asked her where she was getting her tips, but it seemed she had no tips. She simply watched the annual company reports she received, and whenever the report went from black-and-white to full color or became noticeably thicker, she bought; if it got thinner or lost its color, she sold. The lady was using a faculty too few people trust these days—*common sense.* I know of nothing that cuts through more nonsense or gets down to the bottom line more quickly than common sense.

The stock market is, of course, the major gambling arena in business. An outsider's hope of making a fortune in it—with or without measuring the thickness of annual reports—is rather slim, to say the least. True, a fortune is occasionally made on the market, but chances are that this is a result of an inside tip (SEC regulations notwithstanding) rather than a pure lucky break. Therefore, if you're not an expert yourself, do not venture into stocks without a guide. Though even the best broker is not infallible, common sense should tell you that someone who has spent many years studying Wall Street and has a large clientele must be guessing right more times than not. By using him you are tilting the odds in your favor.

And that, after all, is what the habitual winner tries to do in every situation, as a conditioned reflex. None of the real winners I know gamble where chance odds prevail; at most, they make occasional small bets as a momentary diversion. In games where know-how improves the odds, the winner doesn't gamble until he has acquired the knack of tilting the wheel.

Perhaps the most dangerous gamble of all, and another manifestation of negative energy, is business dishonesty. In any career, you can encounter situations where you feel you could get away with cutting a few corners—anything from petty pilfering or shoddy workmanship to selling inferior products at high prices, embezzlement and tax evasion.

Such tactics really are a gamble, and the odds against you are heavy. In the first place, if you get caught, your future may well be in ruins. In the second place, even if you don't get caught, *you* know that you've cheated. That means you've sacrificed your self-respect by admitting you can't win on your own merits. Sooner or later this knowledge will undermine your confidence and thus erode your chances of winning.

Instant destiny is like Russian roulette—you find out immediately if you've won or lost, but in either case you haven't accomplished a thing. Cutting corners is self-defeating—*you can't score at home plate without touching all the bases.*

6. The perils of Ponzi

All right, now you've really taken my words to heart. You're determined to become a winner. You're "getting your act together," you're setting goals for yourself, you're looking around for the big opportunity that will change your life, and you're on your guard against the negative force. Now is the time to beware of the Ponzi scheme. If you let yourself be sucked in, it may dash all your dreams right then and there. It is in your best interest to familiarize yourself with the unmistakable signs of a Ponzi so that you can steer clear of it.

A Ponzi is a plan for creating money out of nothing—that is, nothing but your knowledge of some "foolproof" inside fact, plus the gullibility of others. It's a safe bet that there are a hundred Ponzi schemes in the works right now all over the country and that thousands of investors are throwing their money away on them.

The only people who ever profit from a Ponzi are those who operate it, plus a few small fish who are allowed to make a hundred dollars or so in order to attract the bigger suckers. A few Ponzis are quite frankly dishonest, but most of them hide under the cloak of legality. Some look very respectable, in fact—until you examine the small print.

The art of fleecing the innocent derives its name from what is possibly the biggest and most successful swindle ever perpetrated, a classic dreamed up in 1919 by one Charles Ponzi. An Italian immigrant who had arrived in the United States broke and alone some years before, Ponzi came upon his "inside secret" (there's one in every get-rich-quick scheme) by accident. He ordered something by mail from Spain and got back a coupon that was then being sold abroad by the postal services to encourage overseas mail-order business. The coupon sold in Madrid for a penny (U.S. currency) and was redeemable in the United States for five cents.

Obviously, you could make a four-cent profit on each purchase. Eureka! All you had to do was buy a million coupons and, let's see . . . Suppose a person gives you a penny; you buy the coupon, redeem it, return two cents to the investor (a hundred-percent profit overnight, and no work!), and you still wind up three cents ahead! The staggering possibilities turned Ponzi's head. He quit his job, opened an office and began talking people into investing in his idea. The first to venture a few dollars were of course rewarded within a short time by getting double their money back. Before long, these people convinced others, and money began pouring in. About three months after he started, Ponzi was raking in $250,000 a day. There were lines outside his office, and people were begging him to take their money.

Naturally, as with any such scheme, there was a limit to how long it could be milked before someone got wise. The number of foreign coupons available was not infinite; a hundred or a thousand could be purchased without attracting much attention, but millions and billions—no way! Fortunately for Ponzi, once he had proven to a few hundred people that they could double their money, he no longer had to worry about measly penny coupons. No one checked whether he was really buying them. Thus he was able to fall back on one of the oldest frauds in existence—paying off earlier investors with the money collected from new plungers.

In six months Ponzi collected $10,000,000 (which in 1920 was a unheard-of fortune). Someone eventually blew the whistle and exposed the swindle, but so powerful was the inducement of quick, easy profits that another $5,000,000 found its way into his hands before he found his way to jail. By then, except for the initial few who were paid off to act as bait, the investors were lucky there was enough money in Ponzi's bank accounts to pay them twenty cents on the dollar. Ponzi himself spent years in jail and died in 1949 with total assets of $75.

Anytime you stumble upon something that seems like a magic shortcut to your goal, beware! Pyramid schemes of the Ponzi type have an irresistible lure for the born loser, who always falls for the old "chance to get in on the ground floor" and the "inside track." And then there's the chain letter with promises of instant wealth and fearsome tales of the disasters that will befall anyone who breaks the chain. Old as the hills, and yet these tricks still work!

Right in the heart of Times Square street hustlers still work the old three-card swindle and are apparently doing a brisk business. I expect them to sell the Brooklyn Bridge any day now; the supply of suckers never seems to diminish. The Spanish switch (where your own cash is wrapped up in your presence and you are entrusted to carry it, but what you really have is an identical package containing paper) is evidently still lucrative despite repeated exposure and warnings. Anything that appeals to the little bit of larceny lurking in most of us seems to be revived every few years, always with success.

You may confidently scoff at such simpleminded dodges, which would never take *you* in, but don't forget that similar schemes flourish at every level of sophistication. For each street-corner swindle there is a swindle on the stock exchange or in the government; every group has its quota of suckers.

The only defense against being taken in is your own common sense—which unfortunately is far from common. People don't seem to be able to trust something so clear and simple. But common sense should warn you immediately anytime you run into a deal that looks too good to be true. Is little or no work involved though the rewards are enormous? It's a Ponzi! Does it rely on inside information and promise that lucky you will "get away with murder"? It's a Ponzi, take my word for it.

There is no shortcut to becoming a winner. Yes, you *can* amass wealth rapidly—though not "overnight"—even in this day and age. But you must work hard, know a lot and offer something genuine—a real product, a real service, a real property. There are certain investments that pay off surprisingly well, but again, they must be backed by something solid, not a pipe dream. Whatever that something is, it must actually exist and be available, and it is the buyer's responsibility to see that it is not a phony.

A few years ago, when space flights became a reality, someone started selling lots on the moon—and believe it or not, he did very well. The suckers never inquired how the seller intended to prove ownership—in the unlikely event that he was called on to deliver—or how they would assume title or do anything useful with their imaginary possessions. Perhaps the buyers planned to unload their titles to even bigger suckers at a handsome profit. There's one born every minute, as P. T. Barnum used to say.

Eschew all phonies and get-rich-quick schemes. *There's nothing easy about winning, except that winners can make it look that way!*

7. The tyranny of time

How often have you heard people complain about the things they could accomplish if only they had more time? Perhaps you've even done some moaning along those lines yourself? Of course, time being inflexible, you're stymied, right?

Wrong. There are many ways to overcome time's tyranny. Whenever I hear someone lament that there are only twenty-four hours in a day, I am tempted to present him with a special watch that keeps forty-eight minute hours. Presto! Thirty hours in your day at no extra charge—a full twenty-five percent gain! *Now all you have to do is fill each "hour" with the same amount of activity you used to put into sixty minutes!*

What I'm talking about here is, of course, the basic economic concept of productivity, dramatized so as to bring the abstract idea to life. How do you compress an hour's worth of useful action into forty-eight minutes? By identifying the most nonproductive, time-consuming motions you perform and then doing something to eliminate the waste. Have you noticed, for example, how much of your day you fritter away on the telephone on nonessential business? Find a way to screen your calls, taking only those that tend to produce positive or useful results. If you manage to avoid only one call out of five, you have saved twenty percent of your phone time. And twenty percent of an hour just happens to equal twelve minutes, which is what you must save to meet your "quota."

An article in *Fortune* recently singled out conferences as one of the great time wasters of corporate life. Some companies are apparently installing in their conference rooms display screens that flash on every fifteen minutes, showing the cost of the conference in terms of salaries of all the executives attending. Of course, there are many other ways of squandering time, and most don't require such elaborate corrective measures. Do you write drafts of important letters or memorandums, then go over them with a fine-tooth comb and polish them up? This may produce sparkling prose and perfect punctuation, but it is a waste of time. Learn to do it right the first time; if you know what you want to say, your meaning will come through loud and clear even without the extra polish.

Look for signs of entrenched bureaucratic practices around you. Is the company managed by committees? Is there an automatic reflex to call a meeting every time a minor problem comes up? Do such meetings have a tendency to degenerate into general bull sessions? Is an executive's value measured by the number of memos he can produce on any trivial matter? Does it take reams of forms in quadruplicate to get a pencil sharpener?

If so, you are clearly working in an environment conducive to time wasting. For your own sake, be alert to ways of eliminating wasted motion; you may even find that your suggestions earn you tangible, long-term recognition. I cannot tell you exactly what solutions will work in your particular case, but I can assure you that old-fashioned common sense is a good place to start. Never assume that any business practice, no matter how ingrained, is sacred; many people do things for no better reason than that their predecessors always did them.

In dealing with time, remember that it is a surprisingly elastic commodity if you examine it closely; almost any task tends to fill the time available for it. For example, consider the child who can run to the bathroom, visit the kitchen and make a sandwich, and finally dash into the living room and do a page of homework all in 120 seconds of TV commercials. We all know perfectly well that if the set were not on, the same chores could take the child an hour. The human mind is a wonderfully adaptable thing.

The same holds true in all work. If you have ample time to accomplish a task, you jolly well use all of it. You take a coffee break, write a personal letter, shoot the breeze around the water cooler—and just manage to finish the work on time. If you had been only given a half-hour to do the job, and no buts about it, it would still have been done—very likely just as well, if not better. But of course you would have had to concentrate and allow no distractions, no interruptions, and no idling.

Knowing all this, and relying on your common sense, you can plan your day in forty-eight-minute hours quite easily: just ask yourself how much time you normally take for a unit of work, and then allow yourself only four-fifths of that time to do it. Common sense should also tell you that you cannot carry this procedure to extremes. It is true that if you usually drive to work at fifty-five miles per hour, you can get there in four-fifths of the time by driving at sixty-nine miles per hour—but that is *not* one of the recommended ways of putting time to more effective use!

Besides enabling you to accomplish much more in each working day than you ever did before, the art of compressing time will do you an even bigger favor. It will show you that you can get around the seemingly inexorable laws of the universe, not by attempting to defy them, but by adopting new attitudes toward them. It may not be nice to fool Mother Nature—but it sure is a lot of fun! *And if you can conquer Time, how can anything else stand in your way?*

8. The element of risk

In order to win, you must take risks. The sad thing is that very few people know how. This, I'm afraid, is one of the dubious blessings of our socialization. We know much more about cradle-to-grave security than about risk taking, and more and more people are coming to believe that this kind of government-guaranteed security is a good thing.

I once employed a salesman who seemed to have all the right attributes. He had a gift for persuading others to his point of view, he believed in the product, and he could close sales. I put him on straight commission, and in the first week he compiled an unbelievable record—the best beginning I'd ever seen for a salesman. His check came to more than $800, and that was a number of years ago, when $800 was big money for a week's work.

Next day, I had the surprise of my life. The salesman walked into my office with his wife; they had had a talk the night before, and he simply could not believe that his luck would hold. What if he had a bad week and got no commissions? his wife cried plaintively. What then? And the foolish man offered to work for me just as hard as he had the first week if only I would put him on a straight salary of $150 a week. Needless to say, I let him go; a man who did not believe in himself enough to accept tangible proof of his own ability would eventually fail. He was too busy earning a living to make money! He was asking a pittance for "security" when he had all the real security in the world right there with him all the time: in his heart, in his head, in his soul.

Your ability is your security, the sum total of your experience and your talents. Forget everything else. Don't chase a phantom security that will assure you a measly sum when you retire; if you take a few well-chosen risks now and then, you can do much better than that on your own. Remember, this country was founded by people who had taken the biggest risk of their lives. The 102 people who sailed here on the *Mayflower* faced a huge continent full of unknown dangers. They had given up the security of homes and possessions; they had nothing but their lives, and they risked those, too. In fact, half of them died the first winter. By comparison, how great are the risks you might be asked to take today?

Many a time I've seen good, capable people pass up golden opportunities because they feared a temporary loss of their cozy little security blankets. There's always that one nagging question: Suppose I fail? Do not ask that question; if you do, you are preparing the ground for your failure and conditioning yourself to it. Ask this question instead: Suppose I do not win right off the bat? The answer then becomes obvious: I'll have to make it on the second try or the third. Always remember that one win immediately wipes out a thousand failures and relegates them to total oblivion. The bottom line is always the same: *Winning is everything! Losing is nothing!*

The climb to the dizzy heights of success involves considerable risk taking; you might as well get used to it. You cannot really make it unless you leave the beaten path and strike out into the unknown. The adventurer who faces the wilderness comes back with the hidden treasure! You'll never find it lying in the middle of a well-traveled thoroughfare.

Accepting risks is a part of the winning game—not the blind chance a gambling addict takes but soberly calculated, reasonable risks based on factors over which you have at least some control, where your efforts and abilities come into play. This kind of risk taking, coupled with your desire to win, will produce inevitable victory.

Don't be afraid to go out on a limb—that's where the fruit is!

9. Going broke

One of the main reasons many people hate to take risks and abandon established patterns is that they're afraid of going broke. It's happened to me, and the experience is painful, to say the least. That's because being broke in our success-oriented society is not just a regrettable personal setback; that we could overcome. It is also a social error; a penniless person is shunned like the plague by friend and acquaintance alike. That's the hard part; most of us cannot handle ostracism.

Years ago I became involved in a business project that went bad. After paying off investors from the proceeds of the liquidation I found myself not only broke but saddled with a huge debt. I was sitting in my office brooding when a couple of businessmen arrived for an appointment I had made with them some time before. Assuming that they knew of my misfortune, I was about to tell them it was no use talking, but something in the back of my mind stopped me. Instead, I received them as if nothing had happened, greeted them cordially and invited them to lunch. It turned out they had not yet heard the bad news, and they made me an offer to join them in a venture. I accepted, and in no time at all I was back on my feet again.

Since then I have learned that there are definite cycles in everyone's life. There are times when you hit a slump and everything you try turns out wrong. No one has yet come up with a surefire remedy for such low spots, but one thing is certain: you must ride them out, grin and bear it. Don't become discouraged; don't quit; don't blame your trouble on cosmic forces or your astrological sign or anything else. Even if some such supernatural vibrations are at work, it's a good bet that you could spend a lifetime trying to understand and control them. You can use your time much more fruitfully by simply doing the best you can. If you persist, you will come to a point where everything starts going right and falling into place. No slump lasts for very long unless you give in to it.

The lesson is clear. I got my chance because I did not *act* broke. I did not whine or complain; that would have elicited some sympathy, perhaps, but no offer. I did not look defeated or dejected; that would have assured them I was a loser and made them hold back on the offer they had in mind. I admit I was lucky that they had not yet learned of my recent difficulties. But why should they have? When the reality of my predicament first hit me, I assumed that everyone knew—that my problem was somehow imprinted on me. Such a reaction is natural, but not necessarily appropriate. You'd be surprised how often the people you deal with will not know of your setbacks, at least not right away—if you don't spread the word yourself by acting panicky, that is.

Later on, by the way, my new business associates did learn of my plight, but I acted as if it didn't bother me, so they didn't worry about it either. Of course, it did bother me; I hate to disappoint others or be associated with a failed project. But to the outside world I never showed any signs of distress. It was a matter of private concern, of my personal feelings, and it had no place in everyday business.

If you find yourself broke someday because you've backed the wrong deal, regard it as a delay, not a defeat. To be a winner, you must overcome such delays. Do not waste time on self-pity, brooding, ranting about cruel fate, planning revenge or other useless gestures. Remember the destructive urge, the negative force that lurks within you, striking hardest when you are at your lowest point.

At such times you feel nothing matters anymore; you want to lash out at somebody or something, often innocent bystanders, people you love. You take it out on your dog, your children, your wife. You go on a bender; you become an embarrassment to be with. You either bore people with your tale of woe or insult them irrationally. You suspect them of laughing at you behind your back, of not respecting you anymore, of plotting to get rid of you.

All that is a foolish, utter waste of time. It hurts the people who love you and antagonizes those who know you. Above all, it hurts *you*. It prolongs your agony, slows down the process of bouncing back; sometimes, if you are reckless enough to do or say things that cannot be forgiven, you actually prevent yourself from ever fully recovering.

Never mind all that nonsense! Just imagine for a minute how foolish it will look in retrospect when you have completely re-couped your losses and are going strong. Won't your present despair look ridiculous and self-indulgent? And wouldn't you give a lot to be able to take back some of the idiotic things you did or said when you thought your world was ending? So why say or do them now?

Apart from the effect on yourself and those close to you, in many adverse situations it is objectively better to drive on toward your goal than to retreat. Suppose you have incurred debts in your first business venture. If you return to a regular salaried job it may take you years to get out from under, and then you'll only be back at square one. But suppose you rally, take another chance, and this time, having learned fruitful lessons from your failure, succeed. You'll be in a position not only to repay all you owe but to advance far beyond your present station in life, to be a winner. Isn't it worth a try?

I know many businessmen who have been through the mill, some more than once. Yet today they are winners because they kept their faith and tried again and again. One problem some of them had to face was whether to declare bankruptcy when a project went sour. Naturally, no one likes to go bankrupt; there is unquestionably a stigma attached to it, and many denounce it as the easy, cowardly way out. Practical experience suggests, however-er, that it actually gives you a good chance to score an ultimate victory. Paradoxically, it is also the only course that makes it possible for your creditors to collect one hundred cents on the dollar—although few if any would be willing to listen to this argu-ment.

If you try to be "honest" and square things the hard way, you will find yourself constantly harassed by your creditors—or rather, by their lawyers, who of course must try to justify their fees. You will find your assets attached, and you will be unable to start a new business while you are being hounded for every penny you have. You might eventually pay everyone off this way, but it will certainly take years, and your creditors will not get much return once they pay their lawyers' bills.

Suppose you make a clean break and go into bankruptcy. It does put a black mark on your record, but at least you are free of the pursuing wolves. You can start on the road to recovery immediately. Nine times out of ten, your second try will produce results in a fraction of the time it would take you to set things right without declaring bankruptcy. Once you score, you can ignore all previous debts, but if you are an honest person, you will voluntarily repay whatever you owe. Your creditors will get their money back much faster than if they kept hounding you, and without any middlemen enriching themselves in the process. And they will respect you more.

Like any legislation, bankruptcy law is not perfect. It is sometimes abused to protect outright crooks, and this is regrettable. Still, if the tragedy of a business failure ever faces you, it is often better to resort to bankruptcy than to settle for years of unproductive misery and mediocrity.

10. One of those days . . .

Every one of us has experienced it—I mean the day everything goes wrong from the time you get out of bed to the time you drag yourself, weary and beaten and without having accomplished anything, back home to lick your wounds. Now what? Does this mean you've lost? You're not a winner and never will be?

Absolutely not!

By itself, such a lost day means very little. You can catch up, correct mistakes, set things right the next day or the one after. But much depends on your attitude at the moment of first defeat. Right then and there, it is possible to determine who will eventually turn into a winner and who will stay a loser.

The loser starts blaming. It doesn't matter whom or what he blames. It might be people who acted unexpectedly or contrarily. It might be fate or chance that threw up obstacles. It might be inanimate objects: the car that broke down, the papers that were lost. For all we know, the loser may be right. It could well have been any or all of those things that caused the problem. But it makes no difference. The fact that he is looking outside himself for the blame (and hence the solution) proves that our man is a loser.

This kind of person never wins, because he is expecting the world to smooth his way. If only other people (or things or fate) would shape up, he'd be all right. But of course they never do. After a while, he gets so used to being defeated by that old standby the fickle finger of fate that even if things miraculously fell into place someday he would no longer be able to recognize the opportunity.

The winner, upon finding himself down on the canvas, immediately looks inward—partly for what went wrong (how much of it he has caused by his own oversight, stupidity or ignorance), but mainly, and most importantly, for the solutions. He also knows that the past is already over and cannot be revoked. However, he can and *must* prepare for the future.

Whether things went wrong with or without your unwitting cooperation, only *you* can set them right or take steps to insure that next time you can overcome the problems. To get your motor restarted, reach into your psyche for whatever self-motivators work for you. It may be religion—some people pray at such times, for example—or some little phrase that has meaning for you, such as, "I *know* I am good enough to lick this, and I *will!*" Some people go jogging to collect their thoughts, or do yoga exercises or perhaps just meditate.

Among high-echelon executives there seem to be cyclical trends in crisis-solving methods. At one time, they twirled yoyos; at another time, everyone was doing isometrics; then they all went in for sensitivity training. Fads come and go, but there is never a magic answer. It all comes down to what you believe in, and the one thing a winner always believes in is himself. Anything else is simply a means to help you concentrate, but it is not the solution. The solution is inside you. Whatever the method, use only what suits *you.* Never mind what's fashionable right now; what counts is what's effective.

Once you have used your self-motivators to calm down and start thinking rationally again, analyze your problems. See what went wrong and what you could have done to prevent it, lessen the impact or avert it altogether. If you come to the conclusion that you did make mistakes, store it away for future use. Make sure you learn your lesson; making a mistake once is perfectly natural, but making it twice is inexcusable.

Learning from mistakes is the commonest example of using negative experiences to achieve positive results. Nearly every adversity you meet in life has the potential to yield an equivalent benefit or better—if you apply your imagination to it.

I've already touched on the subject of dissatisfaction and how to use it creatively. Let's say that you have a goal—putting yourself through college, buying a business, etc. To make the money, you have to take an ordinary job like washing dishes in a hash joint. Naturally the job is a bore, and dissatisfaction creeps in. Instead of just getting disgruntled, use each hour you spend on that boring job for something that helps you. For example, you could plan the precise course you will take once you earn enough, and then you won't have to hesitate when the time arrives.

If the drudgery really gets you down, you could try to find ways of speeding up the process. Are there other options, such as jobs that are less objectionable? Is there a way to take the night shift or work overtime to raise your rate of pay? Can you be writing to other prospective employers? Answering ads? Sending out your resumes? What will you say in the covering letter? In this way, you can let your mind work the whole time you are performing routine chores. When you're actively thinking of your interests, you don't have the time or the inclination to brood and become morose about the predicament you are in.

Political prisoners who have endured long years of incarceration invariably credit their survival to the fact that they managed to keep their minds occupied. Many of them have described in detail how they devised elaborate systems of communication, such as rapping on walls, and then spent hours on end relaying messages, playing word games, planning escapes and hatching plots—anything so their minds would not dwell on their hopeless situation.

Alekhine and Bogolyubov did time in adjacent cells in a German prison. They played chess by tapping out the moves. Since they had no chessboards, they had to keep the positions memorized. After many months of this, they became so proficient that upon their release they both rose quickly to the rank of international grand master. Alekhine later became chess champion of the world for eight years. Both men used their minds creatively in adversity.

If such techniques work for people under extreme duress, surely you can manage to get your mind off your own minor setbacks and onto something more inspired. It takes just as much energy to be a loser as to be a winner, believe it or not! Except that the loser impotently squanders his on wasteful emotions like hate, fear, worry, fury and frustration. If the loser had enough common sense to apply the same energy toward positive thoughts and deeds, he could make himself a winner. But for some reason, losers much prefer to dwell on their misery; some virtually wallow in it. Pity them, but never emulate them.

Instead of moping or getting stuck in a rut when problems arise, plan how to bounce back. You need something to occupy your mind at low moments, and there's no bigger challenge or better therapy than the task of designing your comeback. Avoid dramatizing yourself. As far as you are concerned, your setback is a minor incident on the way to the big win. If you look at it this way, others around you will see it in the same light and the whole thing will blow over. People use your own behavior as a clue, so if you act like you've suffered a disaster, they'll take your word for it and start shunning you. If you radiate simple self-confidence and act as if nothing much has happened, they'll accept your behavior at face value and treat you like a winner.

Winners don't cry. They know that next time they'll be able to avoid the pitfalls that thwarted them the last time. To a winner, each reverse is a chance to come back a wiser, bigger person than before.

Anyone who has ever handled a sailboat knows that you can use even adverse winds to get you to your destination. It takes a lot of skill and is much harder and slower going, but the point is that *it can be done!* The same goes in life. Never let adversity go by without gaining something from it.

When things go wrong, the winner still benefits!

11. Emotions

Rage, frustration, euphoria, despair, hate, fear, jealousy, irritation—young and old, we all experience emotions. *The winner learns to control them.*

It's easy to see why. When we express a strong emotion, we are momentarily stripped of the veneer of socially sanctioned conduct. We are, so to speak, in our spiritual underwear—and it isn't easy to command respect in your underwear.

Suppose you've had a disappointing series of meetings all day and you're on edge. You get back to the office five minutes before closing time and discover that your secretary made a typing error in an important letter that has to go out today. It's the last straw; your pent-up emotions give way, and you fly into a rage.

Understandable? Yes, but unwise. Your secretary has not been party to your terrible day. All she knows is that you're making a scene over a trivial matter. How big a man can he be if this trifle bothers him? she wonders. She begins to see you as a loser, she communicates that to others, and your reputation is damaged.

That's why winners control their emotions. They know that frequent or excessive displays of emotion are signs of immaturity and, most important, that they are ineffective. They don't solve problems and they don't get you anywhere.

How would a winner handle the above situation? He would suppress his immediate emotions and try to think in terms of effective action. Is this an isolated error? Is the secretary really good? Then of course he simply points out the mistake and lets her correct it. Is it sloppiness, carelessness or simply lack of ability? Then he considers having her transferred, fired or assigned only such tasks as she is capable of handling. These are actions that get results. Screaming does not accomplish a thing except to make you look small.

When you are faced with unpleasant tasks like dismissing an employee or severing a business relationship, do them in a straightforward way, without rancor. Don't tell someone he's a schemer and a crook and you never want to see him again; just explain that you don't see any profit in further dealings and you therefore wish to discontinue them. After all, he knows what he is; you're not giving him any news.

When emotions are present, reason flees. Hence, a winner would never think of making a major decision or commitment while under the influence of strong emotion. For example, suppose you are experiencing extreme joy; you might be tempted to sign a contract that in a more sober moment you would suspect is not in your best interests. On the other hand, in a fit of anger you might walk out on someone who holds the key to your future.

People who are controlled by their emotions tend to be unreliable, difficult to keep on an even keel, and impossible in a crisis. They often magnify events, and while this may be fine where a happy event is concerned, it tends to have a negative effect in the long run.

Please note that I am speaking here of the *excessive* display of emotions and of the tendency to let emotions *dominate*. I am not putting down emotions per se; to experience them is perfectly human and desirable. The person who expresses no emotions is a zombie and should be avoided at all costs. However, in social situations emotions must be controlled to a reasonable degree. *Emotions exaggerate reality.* They spice life with flavor—but, like spices, they must be used sparingly for best results.

Real winners know how to be both the biggest spendthrifts and the biggest misers, as occasion demands. When experiencing a positive emotion—laughter, happiness, compassion—they recklessly share it with everyone around them. But when beset by negative emotions—fear, hate, misery—they become completely selfish and retire somewhere to stew privately. I firmly believe in this rule—after all, it's only common sense. If I share my joy, everyone benefits; if I share my misery, I cheer myself up only at the expense of depressing others, and that isn't fair to them.

When it comes to expressing your emotions, stay strictly on the sunny side.

12. Popularity

Winners attract people. They are invariably the most popular individuals in any group. They are adulated, emulated, practically worshiped. The phenomenon of hero worship has been with us through the ages, and if you are a winner, you will reap the harvest of this syndrome. You will receive more than your share of flattery, favors, admiration and awe. You will also have to learn to deal with your success. You must separate the sycophants from the sincere admirers, those who want assistance from those who want to bask in reflected glory.

Because of the dearth of leaders in this age of organization men and bureaucrats, people are urgently in need of someone to look up to. As soon as you accomplish anything out of the ordinary, a clique of faithful followers is sure to form around you, like groupies around a rock band or yes-men around a corporate executive.

Winners, beware! If you allow the adoration to get out of hand and turn your head, you may start doing things just to hear the applause of these echo people. They may steer you wrong, suck you into their world, make you lose contact with reality. Do not mistake popularity for success; it's only a by-product. *You have to keep earning your success the way you earned your first win—alone.*

13. The "heresy" of winning

There was a time in the not too distant past when the assertion that winning is everything would not have been open to serious debate. The pioneering mavericks who built this country accepted it as a matter of course, and any major step forward was understood as an all-or-nothing proposition.

That spirit became diluted as time went on, and we now stand just about 180 degrees away from it. A whole generation has been taught to be ashamed of the desire to win. We are constantly being told that materialism is evil, that there is something inherently bad in big business, in being rich, in trying to get ahead of one's neighbor.

As a result, the United States has entered wars without the guts or the will to win them. We have suffered vilification and physical abuse at the hand of all types of punks and hoodlums because we are taught not to throw our weight around. Vacillation has become a virtue, spinelessness is praised as wisdom.

Winning is something of a bad word lately. In schools today, there is a deplorable tendency to downplay the achievers so the nonachievers can have the illusion of equality. Everybody passes everything, everybody is promoted to the next grade, and so on. Listening to the first radio quiz shows, we used to joke that all a contestant had to do was give his name to be declared a winner. Today, most scholastic tests are so blatantly rigged to help every student pass that the joke is no longer funny. There are all sorts of officially sanctioned stratagems designed to put the lazy, the inept and the vicious on an equal footing with the industrious, the bright and the upright.

It's no wonder that the generation brought up under this non-education system misunderstands even such basic truths as the Founding Fathers' concept of equality, which they clearly defined as equality of opportunity. The fashion today is to pretend that they meant such absurdities as equal income for all, guaranteed by the government. Naturally, this state of affairs can be achieved only by taking hard-earned money from those who have some-how managed to break through the demoralizing equality barrier and distributing it among those who think it's nobler to receive. And wouldn't you know it, such a scheme is in effect. It is called progressive taxation—the government's way of telling you that earning good money is evil and must be punished.

What this does to the perfectly normal human impulse to excel and to win in the game of life can easily be imagined. Why should you struggle to make your fortune when you know it will be taken away from you to subsidize the loafer and the parasite? If you are a member of one of the favored minorities, the demoralizing effects of this system are even worse. If you're inclined to be lazy, you know you don't have to exert yourself, because everything will be handed to you on a silver platter through "affirmative action." If you are ambitious and hardworking, you are deprived of the joy of winning, because everyone naturally assumes you got where you are only by favored treatment—the implication of affirmative ac-tion being that its beneficiaries are unable to make it on their own. It is a sad indication of the extent of the disease that an over-whelming majority of blacks and other minorities favor affirmative action (in other words, cheating in their favor) without realizing how it insults the honest and capable achievers among them. A marvelous example of the results of consistent brainwashing!

What all this means to you personally is that if you want to be a winner, you must first of all have a philosophical basis for your action. Use logic and common sense to rediscover the truth that to work for your own betterment with a desire to win is not shameful or evil, no matter how many politicians declare it to be so. Realize that the stigma attached to success is a smokescreen created solely for the purpose of justifying ever higher taxes. The politician is goaded at every step by masses of have-nots who clamor for free handouts. The only way he can get elected by these leeches is to promise them their feast, and the only way he can deliver on the promise is to siphon more and more money away from the few who still have some. Naturally he must create an atmosphere in which such arrant extortion somehow appears justifiable.

Keep this firmly in mind while setting your personal goals. Make sure you never let anything or anyone persuade you to feel guilty about making a success of yourself, striking it rich or creating a business empire. The minute you start believing the bleeding hearts, you're lost. The feeling of guilt about being better off than the other fellow will rob you of essential motivation and the desire to win, and you'll never make it. *Remember, it takes iron determination and total self-confidence to win.* That's what you are concerned with, and nothing else.

Furthermore, do not hesitate to use every possible legal method to maximize your income and profits. Creative bookkeeping, foreign transfer of assets, and whatever else is legally permissible is not cheating but pure self-defense. You are protecting what is yours for the best reason of all—because you have earned it. The government wants to take it away from you to finance insane and inefficient services benefiting no one, and it's the government that is immoral, not you.

Using every possible tax loophole, for example, is not just helpful but is in many cases an absolute prerequisite for staying in business at all. There are so many rules penalizing businesses that the time is fast approaching when one hundred percent taxation will be technically possible. As you may remember, Swedish director Ingmar Bergman had to leave his own country recently because some idiot bureaucrat, diligently applying all the laws at his command, declared that Bergman's income should be taxed at 103%. In other words, not only would he not be allowed to keep a penny of each million dollars he earned, but he would be penalized $30,000 for having earned it!

Although we have not yet reached this point of utter bedlam, the general direction is clearly indicated. Zealous bureaucrats daily devise new rules and regulations, and any businessman attempting to be scrupulously honest about paying all the required taxes would promptly go out of business. Besides, the rules are predicated on the assumption that you will cheat; no government official expects for a second that anyone would comply with the rules voluntarily, and therefore the system is rigged so that you wind up paying the IRS something no matter what you do. To help them rob you by giving a naively complete account of your finances is not patriotic so much as moronic. Going broke does not help the country; quite the contrary.

Let's make things perfectly clear: it is in *your* best interest and ultimately also in *your country's* (even if the fools in Washington have temporarily lost sight of the fact) that you:

1. make as much money as you possibly can;
2. keep as much of it as you can legally manage;
3. *win* and succeed in spite of current propaganda against such heretical behavior!

The only restriction that applies here is that you cannot make your fortune at the expense of other people's freedom and rights. In other words, don't be a crook and don't climb on anyone else's back (but this is only common sense; you really don't need such an admonition). Other than that, anything goes. As writers from Ralph Waldo Emerson to Robert Ringer have pointed out, *looking out for Number One is really the most sane, rational and moral thing you can do in this world.*

Never let your initiative be diluted, deflected or turned off by political doubletalk or sociological hogwash. If the game is played by nonsensical rules, learn them and learn how to beat them, just as you would any other handicap. Never take or believe anything from those who seek to weaken you, sap your strength, slow you down or spoil your victory. Do not pause to give a hand to the guy in the gutter; he does not want to rise to your level but to drag you down to his.

Winning means to be gloriously, triumphantly selfish. Self-reliant.

Interested in promoting your status, wealth and well-being. Determined to make yourself and your family free, strong and independent. And there can never be anything wrong with that, no matter what anyone says.

14. Equality vs. equal opportunity

In recent years, a lot of political fervor has been generated by the issue of equal opportunity—for blacks, gays, women, the foreign-born and countless other groups. Color-blind Estonian dwarfs will probably be next. All this is fine as long as nobody makes the mistake of confusing equal opportunity with actual equality.

Nature abhors equality; hence efforts invoking such a perversion of natural laws are doomed in the long run. Ions have either positive or negative energy; if you make them all equal you have only dead matter—nothing at all. Living creatures interact with one another; some devour others, some live off others, and all of them fight for their share of food, shelter, mates and territory. Competition, survival of the fittest—all that exists in nature. But equality? Not a chance.

A government that used common sense would make sure that everyone had the same opportunity: the same chance to obtain education, the same chance to get work, the same legal protection, etc. Beyond that, it's up to the individual. Some will make more of their opportunities than others; that is to be expected. Some will be winners, some losers; that's the way it should be. That's what this book is all about.

Attempting to "correct" this natural state of affairs is ridiculous. Some people, given their natural proclivities, will wind up rich, some will wind up poor; trying to equalize them through a tax system that soaks the rich and pampers the poor is nothing but an attempt to make angels out of people—the utopian dream so dear to the heart of every politician. It will never work, and it shouldn't. There is no justice in it; it subsidizes laziness, obtuseness and arrogance while penalizing brains, effort and diligence. No country can afford to mistreat its best citizens and hope to survive. Everyone will be truly equal only when national income, GNP and all other economic indicators reach zero. Then you'll have the only kind of complete equality that exists in nature: death.

In 1945 an interesting social experiment took place in Czechoslovakia. During the war, many black marketeers and collaborators had made fortunes, and the exile government, upon returning to the country after the German defeat, realized that these traitors would enjoy an enormous financial advantage over the honest patriots. It therefore abruptly canceled all bank balances and issued new currency. Each citizen received five hundred units of the new money.

What could have been more just, equitable and perfect? Equality had been achieved in modern times! Or had it? Within days, there were people throwing around thousands and others begging for pennies. Within a month, the country had its first new millionaire. The dream of equality was just that—a dream. Natural laws took over from would-be meddlers and restored *the proper state of inequality.*

Actually, the Czech government did the right thing: it gave everyone an equal chance, but it did not declare that everyone should stay at the same level. Those who quickly lost their shares did so knowingly, at their own risk; no one held a gun to them. Those who quickly accumulated the new money were the same ones who would always have money in a free enterprise system, no matter what the circumstances. The winners won, the losers lost; it's as simple as that. Rarely has it been demonstrated with such crystal clarity and in such a short time that the tendency towards inequality always asserts itself in any social situation.

You don't want to be equal to your neighbor, you want to be better. He, I warrant, is hoping to do better than you—and more power to him if he can. You wouldn't feel comfortable if you knew that at the end of the year someone would come around to compare your incomes and hand the difference to whoever earned less. Yet that's exactly what the politicians are trying to sell us, except that they're much more circumspect about it and talk in terms of the "disadvantaged" and other such tripe!

Never strive for equality. What you want is opportunity. *Enforced equality guarantees universal mediocrity.*

15. Overcoming handicaps

When it comes to overcoming handicaps, human resourceful-
ness and ingenuity are nothing short of marvelous. David overcame a huge disparity in size to fell Goliath, Demosthenes overcame a speech defect to become the most renowned orator in
ancient Greece, and so on down through history. One of the most
spectacular examples of all is the miracle of Helen Keller.

Such triumphs continue right to this day. Not long ago on a
television program I saw two brothers who had independently
amassed fortunes despite the fact that they were both four-foot
midgets. Glenn Turner became a successful entrepreneur despite an extra share of problems, including a harelip. People who
bounced back after a crippling attack of polio are legion, from
singer Jane Froman to President Franklin Roosevelt. Losing a leg
did not stop Pegleg Bates from dancing, or Monty Stratton from
pitching in the major leagues.

Handicaps that are social, political or psychological rather than
physical yield equally well to determination and persistence. The
Minneapolis tycoon Percy Ross failed in a dozen businesses and
became something of a social leper in credit circles; but in 1959
he managed to find backers for one more venture, the plastics
business, and within five years he was a millionaire. Freddy Laker
dreamed of providing cheap air transportation at a time when the
British airline industry had been nationalized, making it impossible for private enterprise to break in. Not being smart enough to
know this, he went to court against the government twice, won his
case, got his planes into the air, and single-handedly stood the
airline business on its ear—and this despite opposition from gov-

ernment bureaucrats in a deadly alliance with British and American airlines, who did not want their prices undercut.

Laker dared to charge less than $200 for nonstop flights from London to New York or Los Angeles—a price he set in 1975 and continues to charge even in 1980, when everything else has gone through five years of two-digit inflation. Before he came on the scene, the airline business was a cost-plus proposition pure and simple. No one cared much what the costs were since they could simply be passed on to the consumer with an added ten percent for profit. But Laker forced the airlines to be competitive and cut costs. They had to come somewhere near his price, or he would have wound up with all the business. As it was, starting from nothing, he carried twenty-five million passengers in his second year. He proved that airline prices can be reasonable without sacrificing the comfort or safety of the passengers. He also overcame all kinds of obstacles placed in his path by his own government.

There is another major class of "handicaps" designed by certain social scientists to fit into their pet theories. They are really not handicaps at all and in fact should sometimes be classified as the exact opposite. A favorite of the bleeding hearts is "adverse environment," meaning a background of poverty, a slum childhood or a broken home. This illusory concept persists despite the clear evidence of thousands of achievers, from show business giants to Supreme Court judges, from business magnates to respected scientists, who can point to a childhood on the wrong side of the tracks.

To me, nothing constitutes a more powerful incentive than precisely this kind of environmental handicap. I experienced the bone-chilling, grinding poverty of Appalachia in my own childhood, and it was this firsthand knowledge that gave me the will and determination to get out of there at any cost and become a winner. So don't come crying to me if you're among those officially classified as "disadvantaged." Consider yourself lucky to have an edge on everyone else because of your excellent incentive to improve your lot. Contrary to popular opinion, it's often the members of the privileged classes who are truly handicapped.

They face the grave problem of finding a worthwhile purpose in life.

As to such alleged handicaps as race, sex, religion or nationality, they may sometimes slow you down or force you to use your ingenuity, but they can also motivate you to escape your seemingly inevitable fate. If you're sound of mind and heart, the incentive more than outweighs the drawbacks.

"Being a Negro is not a disgrace in this country, but it is damn inconvenient," Bert Williams said somewhat before the turn of the century. At the time racial equality was not even being whispered about, let alone seriously discussed. And yet this fine black entertainer climbed all the way to the top of his profession, making an unprecedented break into all-white vaudeville and earning universal respect. Paul Robeson won fifteen varsity letters at Rutgers and became that college's first All-American for two successive years, 1917 and 1918—a time when blacks in athletics were nothing but a rumor. Louis Armstrong was both black and an orphan, but he became the most famous jazz musician of all time. Thurgood Marshall was black and poor, and he became a Supreme Court justice. Today any black who can look at such accomplishments and claim that his race is slowing him down is simply using it as a crutch.

If you are a woman, do you think your sex keeps you from being a winner? Humbug! From Cleopatra to Madame Curie, women who had what it took made their mark on the world without worrying about whether they were "liberated" or not. Amelia Earhart became an ace pilot in the 1920s, though flying was considered a very unladylike occupation at the time. Alice Guy directed films in 1896, when Cecil B. De Mille was still in knee pants. If Joan of Arc could lead an army in 1429, if Dr. Mary Edwards Walker could win a Congressional Medal of Honor in 1865, if Mary Baker Eddy could launch the Christian Science movement in 1875, how can you seriously think of your sex as a handicap in the 1980s?

National origin is another handicap that's more imaginary than real. The achievements of some of the millions of immigrants who came to these shores are too well known to need repeating.

From Louis B. Mayer to Albert Einstein, from Enrico Caruso to Henry Kissinger, immigrants who had the spark in them overcame prejudices, language barriers and every other obstacle to emerge as winners. Daniel Inouye, a World War II hero and United States senator from Hawaii, is a Japanese-American and has only one arm besides. Anastasios Kyriakid, a Greek, came here in the late 1960s without a dime to his name and without a word of English. His case proves that a handicap can actually be turned to advantage. He was so irked by his language problem that he worked out the idea for a computerized translating lexicon, and he now controls a company with a $10,000,000 backlog of orders for his gadget.

Other, less obvious handicaps can also be overcome if you are a winner. You might think that a leading lady has to have beauty and sex appeal, but Bette Davis and Katharine Hepburn made the grade without fitting conventional definitions of these qualities. Fanny Brice was homely as could be and still performed as a headliner in the glamor-conscious Ziegfeld Follies. Marie Dressler looked like a battleship and was a top star in theater and films. Ben Turpin actually had his crossed eyes insured by Lloyds of London against accidental uncrossing.

Show business is full of successful people who overcame all sorts of handicaps. Joe E. Lewis had his throat cut and was left for dead by gangsters; despite his ruined vocal chords, he became a top-notch comedian; in England, actor Roger Livesey overcame a similar vocal chord injury. Wingy Mannone was a one-armed trumpet player; Sammy Davis, Jr., and Peter Falk are one-eyed; Totie Fields and Jimmy Savo both stayed in show business despite the loss of a leg. Michael Flanders was confined to a wheelchair, but he teamed up with Donald Swann to put on *At the Drop of a Hat,* a show that enjoyed an eight-year run all over the world. Mel Tillis is a major country recording star despite his stutter. Yul Brynner accepted his baldness and turned it into an asset. Harold Lloyd had a mangled hand, yet he specialized in acrobatic feats in his films. The accomplishments of blind entertainers—Ray Charles, Stevie Wonder, José Feliciano—would fill a book.

As we have noted, the term *handicap* is not restricted to physical shortcomings. There are many fine gradations and subjective interpretations of what constitutes a handicap. The only defining feature of a handicap is that it lowers your chances of success through no fault of your own and is therefore something to be overcome.

I know a very dear lady whose original home was Cleveland, and who married a Southerner and moved to Atlanta in the 1940s. She aspired to a high social standing, and finding that the cream of local society was invariably listed in something called the *Atlanta Blue Book,* she determined to get herself between its covers. Everyone agreed that she was wasting her time. This particular publication, she was informed, was a purely arbitrary selection made by ultra-snobbish Dixie chauvinists to whom any Yankee was anathema. You had to be born a Southerner to qualify for the human race at all, and preferably you should come from a family that had lived in the South since before the *Mayflower.*

My friend ignored all this. She settled in a huge antebellum mansion and joined every social club in town. She supported the Art League, the Cyclorama, the DAR and dozens of other causes. She played bridge, attended kaffeeklatsches arranged flower shows. She acquired a Southern accent and dropped references to the Civil War in her conversations. She volunteered to take children to the Kennesaw Mountain and Stone Mountain parks. She steeped herself in local history, went to lectures and prowled museums.

The incredible happened: after some twenty-five years of being frostily ignored, she suddenly found herself a genuine *Blue Book* blueblood! It is not for me or anyone else to judge whether the result was objectively worth the effort. You and I may think that having your name printed in someone's list of eligibles is utterly meaningless, but the point is that *she* wanted it, *she* considered it important, and *she* overcame a virtually insurmountable obstacle to get it. The lady is and always will remain a winner in my book; she set a hard goal and attained it. That's what counts, and that's the only thing that counts.

Do you still say her effort was wasted? Consider: she became a charming hostess; she acquired a fine knowledge of art, history and Southern folklore; she filled her house with precious antiques; she gave countless hours and substantial monetary support to many worthy charities; she instilled in her three fine children a sense of pride and a patriotic awareness; she gained access to the intellectual, political and artistic circles in her area. How could such accomplishments be anything but good? Her work toward her goal made her happy and fulfilled. A winner if ever I saw one!

The bottom line is this: *handicaps, no matter what their type or severity, are there to be overcome.* The real achievers of this world do not need their rights assured by laws or decrees. They never did, nor do they now, require equal rights amendments, human rights legislation, racial or national quotas or any other artificial boost. They went ahead and became winners by their own efforts. They never asked the government for favored treatment or handouts. They never appealed to anyone for sympathy, special privileges, tax exemptions or other gimmicks. All they asked was to be allowed to stand on their own talents and do what they knew best.

None of the above implies disapproval of governmental or civic measures taken in the interest of equalizing opportunities. It is merely my intention to point out the clear and obvious fact that the existence or nonexistence of such protection has never made an iota of difference to those who were really determined to reach their goals.

Do not regard handicaps as insurmountable obstacles. Instead, use them constructively as an added incentive.

III

THE WINNERS' CIRCLE

1. Winning in business

The best and most thrilling way to become a winner is still, thank heaven, the private enterprise route—although the government, through a maze of insane bureaucratic regulations, appears to be doing its best to stifle initiative. But that in itself has become part of the game. The challenge today is not just to get your enterprise off the ground but to keep it alive in spite of virtually certain interference by Big Brother's bumbling buzzards.

The first thing you need is a sound idea. You may think that will stop you right off the bat—it certainly takes a genius to think up an idea, and you're no genius, right? Don't you believe it! Not being anything like a genius myself, I can assure you that most of the so-called brilliant ideas in business are based on plain, ordinary common sense.

Take the case of Fred Sands. As a young man growing up in California, he noticed that the cost of building a new home was steadily creeping up. Projecting five or ten years ahead, he could see that the cost of new construction would be so prohibitive that comparatively few people would be able to afford it. What could be more logical than to conclude that the price of existing houses would skyrocket accordingly? People would certainly leap at the opportunity to save by buying an older house rather than paying through the nose for a new one.

There is nothing particularly startling in this reasoning; it's the sort of conclusion you or I could arrive at just as easily. In fact, many a time we have probably done so at home or at a gathering. The only difference is that Fred Sands backed his conviction with deeds. He started a real estate business specializing exclusively in existing houses in good neighborhoods.

As he predicted, their price shot up out of all proportion, as much as thirty percent a year for a period of several years. He started from scratch at the beginning of the 1970s, and in ten years he had opened ten branches and was employing four hundred people. By the end of the decade, houses he had acquired for $40,000 were selling for anywhere between $500,000 and $1,000,000 depending on the neighborhood and the quality of the house. Fred Sands became one of the biggest realtors in southern California, a multimillionaire, and living proof of the fact that it takes no superbrain to succeed—*just a person with an idea and the guts to back it up.*

Or take Orville Redenbacher, the popcorn king. As an agriculture student at Purdue, he took part in hybridization experiments that produced a superior strain of popping corn yielding almost perfect results, with no "old maids" (unpopped kernels) left in the pan. The experiments were certainly interesting, and most of the students duly admired the wonders of crossbreeding. Then they went home and grew the same old types of popping corn; after all, it was selling and it was good enough.

But not good enough for Orville. He reasoned that if the popcorn-buying public knew there was no need to lose a percentage of kernels in each batch of popcorn, they would buy his superior strain. He began to grow it and invested in a publicity campaign to convince people of the difference in popcorns. Within a few years, Orville Redenbacher Gourmet Popcorn swept the market. In 1979 he grossed about $40,000,000 in popcorn sales. Not bad for a man who started with a few acres, an idea *and a conviction.*

I cannot stress the importance of conviction strongly enough. You must be convinced that your idea is sound and then act on it. Just think how many thousands of students had taken the same course at Purdue and seen the same superior hybrid! Any one of them could easily have reasoned that this popcorn would outsell other types if it was produced on a large scale and marketed properly. I'm sure many did just that. The trouble is, they left it there. Orville succeeded because he took action; he believed in the idea and in himself (which is really one and the same thing) enough to do something about it. That is one of the crucial differences between losers and winners. *Winners act; losers wish they had.*

Too many people want to cling to the security of a steady paycheck and have entrepreneurial opportunities as well. You cannot have both—at least not under ordinary circumstances. If you have an idea and a conviction, nine times out of ten you must go out on a limb and leave your cozy job. You must start hustling, put your idea across to others, persuade, cajole, argue and convince. You must organize your business and get it going.

Start taking chances and betting on yourself. The only way to take advantage of the few remaining opportunities in the free enterprise system is to plunge in. There's no easy step-by-step introduction, so don't waste your time looking for one. It's strictly a sink-or-swim proposition, and you must take the leap when you think the time is ripe.

2. Jumping on the bandwagon

If you've been racking your brain in vain for an original idea, perhaps you've reached the conclusion that it would be much easier to jump on a bandwagon that's already rolling. Fine, but be aware of two drawbacks: there's a danger of picking a "bandwagon" that's anything but; and even if you've got the right idea, the odds are against your getting anywhere near as rich as its originator.

As to "bandwagon identification," we can find no better illustration than the television industry, where even the palest carbon copy of a successful show seems to be preferred to an original thought. In 1955 *Gunsmoke* premiered, and it was a smashing success. Immediately every producer in town assumed that the public wanted Westerns, and scores of them cropped up all over the tube. With one or two notable exceptions, such as *Bonanza* (which, however, did not arrive until years later), they all died a quick death. The copy boys had the wrong trend. The public did not want Westerns as such; they liked *Gunsmoke* because it was a damn good show.

In the 1930s Parker Brothers put Monopoly on the market, and it sold phenomenally. Copies appeared by the dozen, but Monopoly is still here while all the other games died on the sales counter. Similarly, in the late 1940s, when Selchow and Righter came out with Scrabble, imitators assumed that the trend was word games. A whole slew of word games went on the market, and even Selchow and Righter tried a few variants on the basic formula, but none of them scored anywhere near the success of

Scrabble. It just happens to be a superior family game, and that's what sold the public.

To identify a trend properly, you must make sure that it is generic and not a one-shot thing. For example, electronic games you can play on your television set represent a genuine trend, and so do video cassettes. All kinds of them are eagerly accepted by the public. But even if you have properly identified a trend, that does not assure success. Naturally, whoever came up with the original idea has it properly protected, and if you try to peddle an imitation, however well disguised, you can be sure he'll be after you with all the lawyers he can buy. Wouldn't you do the same in his place?

Finally, even if you have an idea that's original as far as you're concerned, step carefully. Someone may have "stolen" it from you before you were even born! A friend of mine once took his children to a miniature golf course on a cold day. Watching them play in the inclement weather, he idly mused that if the course was covered it would be much nicer. Wait a minute! Wouldn't it also enable the place to operate all year, instead of just in the summer? The more he thought about it, the surer he was that he had a million-dollar idea. He approached some potential backers, and they were all enthusiastic. Fortunately, he had the sense to have an attorney look into it before he went any further. As it turned out, someone had not only had the idea years before but had gotten a patent and was selling year-round enclosed miniature golf courses on a franchise basis. My friend assures me he had never seen one of these, and I have no reason to doubt him, so the idea really was original in his mind.

This story goes to show that whatever the human mind can conceive has probably already been thought of by others. The only question is whether anyone has taken steps to do something about it. If they have, there's only one thing to do: go on to something else. Of course, if you feel you have come up with a substantial improvement on the basic idea, you can always offer to join the existing organization. Better yet, you can enter the field as a competitor. In the latter case, you should make a deal with the owner of applicable patents, copyrights, etc. It's cheaper in the long run than facing years of court wrangles over possible in-fringements.

If you're sure you have properly identified a bandwagon and you're aware of the abovementioned pitfalls, then there's nothing wrong with jumping on. You must expect, of course, that others will do the same and that it will be harder to make a killing than it would be with a new idea of your own. However, in view of the fact that a truly revolutionary idea comes up at the rate of perhaps one per decade, it's better to be realistic.

Even if you cannot be completely original and are joining an established field, you can still be a winner if you give it all you have. With enthusiasm, vigor and an unprejudiced mind, you can impart a distinctive flavor, come up with an imaginative approach or a new twist that will make the difference. It's only natural that we all prefer to be innovators. However, let's not lose sight of the fact that *a successful imitator is far better off than an original thinker whose idea fails to pay off.*

3. Business partnerships

Two heads are better than one. It should follow that if you join a partner in a business enterprise, you are doubling your chance of success. In point of fact, you are cutting it in half!

No matter what the theory says, in practice I have found that partnerships consist of two or more individuals who are afraid to take full responsibility for a decision. As a result, each waits for the other to take the first step, until it is either too late to take advantage of an opportunity or the decision is reached under pressure at the last minute. Later, when it becomes clear that the decision was the wrong one—as such hasty ones often are—each partner invariably blames the other.

In dealing with a partnership, you will find yourself waiting interminably for a clear answer or a definite commitment. Nothing can be done until the partners are in accord, and one of them is always out of town or busy with something else, so that the matter must be postponed. If one of them favors your proposition, the other is sure to oppose it on principle; if one of them gives you a firm commitment, the other one tries to find grounds for canceling it.

If you are involved in partnership, then you're in for some rough sledding. If you divide the responsibilities along clear-cut lines, each of you will think he got the worst part of the job; if you split everything down the middle, you will wind up consulting each other about whether to buy another box of staples and hating each other's guts.

It's a little like rowing a boat; one person can do it perfectly well, but if two combine their efforts, each invariably reaches the conclusion that the other is nothing but a hindrance and is not pulling a fair share of the load. Discord is almost inevitable; to achieve true coordination would require years of precision training. This is true even in calm waters. In inclement weather a boat operated by two people is twice as likely to capsize as a one-man craft. In a panic situation, even years of training sometimes do not prevent partners from failing to coordinate or to anticipate each other's actions correctly.

I am not here to tell you that partnerships do not work at all or that they cannot be made to succeed in some circumstances. It's just that I have seldom encountered one that was a real winning combination and that enhanced each partner's chances for personal fulfillment. Still, there are cases where a business partnership can thrive. Say, for example, that you have joint ownership of a cab; one person drives it days, the other nights. This arrangement can work out perfectly provided that each partner is satisfied with the assigned hours and doesn't start claiming that the other has a better deal.

Partnerships are particularly apt to work in small businesses like accounting practices or candy stores. In most cases, successful partnerships are those in which the business can be made more profitable by longer hours, more than a single person can handle. Then a partner can ease the burden, and a working symbiosis can evolve. Many lawyers, doctors and other professionals form partnerships that are successful and profitable for all concerned. They can share the rent on a building or set of offices, provide a wider range of services than would be possible for an individual, and cover for each other during vacations or absences. Again, this can work out quite well if there is no overlapping of interests or competition for clientele.

But in entrepreneurial businesses, where frequent decisions based on individual judgment must be made, where management necessarily involves some risk taking, partnerships have a tendency to make everyone less daring and hence less likely to grab a winning opportunity by the tail. Theoretically, partners should reinforce each other; in practice, each partner feels he is being slowed down or barred from total success by that blockhead he's tied up with. Ideal, symbiotic partnerships, like communism, exist only in the abstract; any attempt to put them into effect with real people breaks down swiftly and disastrously.

A partnership is much more vulnerable than an individual enterprise. If you make a mistake in your own business, it will cost you some money and time, and that's probably all there is to it. If you make a mistake in a partnership, you have an excellent chance of winding up in court, with accusations, recriminations and invective flying around like feathers in a pillow fight. In fact, I wouldn't be surprised if partnerships as a way of doing business were invented by idle lawyers who wanted to assure themselves of steady work. It's a rare partnership that can survive a setback without a few legal vultures feeding on its decaying carcass.

If you want to be a winner, stay away from commercial partnerships.

4. Winning and social relations

In social life as in everything else, *winners attract winners*. If you adopt winning attitudes in your own life, you will soon find that your circle of contacts is widening. You will find new friends and romantic partners who are attuned to winning and will respond to your heightened sensibilities. You yourself will now feel more responsive to people who have similar ambitions and are oriented to winning. You will take sustenance from their drive, and they will derive pleasure from yours. The winners' circle is a mutually supportive society.

As you raise your sights, you may discover that some of your old friends are drifting away. They are the ones who have little ambition beyond mere survival, the ones who always gripe and get tangled up in trivial matters. You may start to lose patience with them, and they may start to bore you. This process is nothing to be alarmed about; some people stop at a given stage of personal development, others go beyond. The weeding out is natural, and such people will be just as happy to drop you as you are to drop them! Your new friends will more than compensate for the loss.

As you develop the self-confidence that is the mark of a true winner, you will find that you are also having an easier time in business and other formal dealings with people. Take a typical situation in a highly competitive corporate unit. An executive of ordinary ability and ambitions is usually nervous and subservient in the presence of higher authority, defensive among colleagues at his own level (because he suspects them, probably rightly, of trying to surpass him for promotion), and domineering and arro-

gant toward subordinates (lest they wise up to him and undermine his authority). At no time can such a person afford to be
caught off guard. That way lie nervous tensions, ulcers, and in
extreme cases strokes and heart attacks.

The winner, by contrast, knows he will get ahead in life, no
matter what is going on around him. He does not envy superiors
since he is confident that his turn will come soon; hence he can
deal with the higher-ups in a fearless and straightforward fashion
(which, incidentally, wins more respect than our nervous friend's
kowtowing and obsequiousness).

The winner can be friendly and open to those on his own level
in the hierarchy. He need not worry that one of them may earn a
promotion before he does, since his own plans are already far
more ambitious than climbing another little rung up the corporate ladder. Thus he can in all sincerity wish his colleagues the
best of luck. A real winner does not begrudge others the chance
to win; on the contrary, he rejoices in their success.

To the people in lower echelons, the winner can afford to be kind
and thoughtful. He has the security of knowing where he is going
and how he will get there, and he feels neither threatened nor
compromised if he deals with them on a perfectly equal basis. As
a result, he is able to delegate authority effectively. He makes no
attempt to hoard it all for himself; he is happy to see others use
their initiative. Far from detracting from his own authority, they
are making it easier for him to discharge his duties and concentrate more of his energies on his major goal.

Thus the winner, even during the temporary daily grind,
already sets himself apart from the run-of-the-mill nonentity. He
respects power but is not overawed by it; he knows he will wield it
himself one day. He never covers up mistakes, never runs scared,
never hesitates to share credit or shoulder blame. He is willing to
assume responsibility; given a choice, he will always prefer making a decision to passing the buck. Winning is mostly a matter of
making the right decisions anyway, so you might as well start
making them wherever you are!

In social situations, you can tell the winners by the way they
assert their leadership, even without consciously trying to do so.

They invariably dominate a group, control the subject of conversation and influence the group's actions. Most winners possess above-average language skills and can get their meaning across clearly and succinctly.

Effective communication is a prerequisite of winning. If you stammer or hesitate, if it takes you too long to put your thoughts into words, if you don't know how to make a point and get others to accept your views, you are laboring under severe handicaps. A winner not only needs confidence in himself but must also be able to inspire it in others. This is extremely hard to do without the help of skillful communication. If you have the floor, speak assertively and emphasize positive values. *Speak out, speak positively, radiate confidence,* and you have the makings of a winner in all social relations.

5. Winning and love

Love is irrational. This quality adds greatly to its excitement and charm but also makes it hard to understand. Many otherwise successful people fail in their love lives because they do not fully appreciate this irrationality.

Love cannot be treated like a commodity. In love, it's the imitation you pay for, the real thing that's free. Yet if you have any sense you'll value love more highly than anything in this world.

You cannot *make* anyone love you, no matter how forceful or persuasive you are. Quite often, the more you push the less response you get. As a winner, you must be a realist above all; therefore you must recognize the special characteristics of the love game and make sure you don't play it by the wrong rules.

You can earn another person's love, but not in the aggressive way you earn money in business. It's primarily a question of taking a spark that's already there and kindling it into a flame. But the spark must be alive in both partners; one-sided, unrequited love, however strong, is a sheer waste of time and leads only to heartache.

Love suspends the normal rules of quid pro quo—preferred consideration for products or services rendered. You do not receive love for anything particular you give or do; rather, love is a continuous process of giving and taking in which there can never be an accurate accounting. Love is a voluntary gift, and the only way to "win" it, in the final analysis, is simply by being yourself. *Therefore the only path to winning in love is to allow the other person to know your real self.*

If you believe in the adage "All's fair in love and war," you are deluding yourself. Any trickery or subterfuge, such as presenting yourself in a better light than you really deserve, can only work temporarily. It may lead to momentary liaisons and quite a bit of physical bliss, but it doesn't last. If you plan to enter a permanent relationship like marriage, any misrepresentation is fatal. Sooner or later, your true nature will emerge, and your lies will become a bone of contention and ruin everything.

If you find yourself striking out with a person after you've given the relationship you're best shot, move on. You can win in love, but you cannot do it alone. You must find a willing accomplice. And once you have someone's love, you can keep it only by continuing to be worthy of it; there is no other protection. Any attempt to possess or lock away love as if it were your personal property will only put it to flight.

Jealousy is the prime example of this point—possessiveness at its worst. It kills love just as surely as a deliberate attempt to hurt. A show of jealousy betrays inner insecurity, a sure sign of a loser. If you have grounds for your suspicions, jealousy will speed up the departure of your partner. Worse, if you have no reason to worry, jealousy can *cause* your partner to consider straying . . . and from there it's but a short step to action.

Money is another form of possession, and its relationship to love is complex. We all know money cannot buy love, but we also know it can secure some very attractive facsimiles. When you see an aging tycoon squiring a flashy starlet bedecked with jewels, or a wealthy dowager accompanied by a muscle-bound stud, you know it's not a love match but a simple business arrangement. They know they're not fooling anyone, too; what they are really doing is showing a tangible proof of success. The attractive young companion is the equivalent of a Rolls-Royce, a yacht or a big mansion—and probably lots more fun. It's only human nature to want to display the fruits of success, but the danger lies in the delusion that company and services, and maybe even a certain amount of loyalty—albeit purchased—equal love.

In many cases, successful people are quite satisfied with such substitutes. Perhaps love is not their game; winning in other fields may take priority over personal attachments, or there may be other reasons for leaving love out of the picture. If so, there is no problem.

On the other hand, some people believe in principle that they cannot be winners unless they sacrifice their personal lives, and for that reason they do not assume the responsibilities of a relationship or a family. This is nonsense. There is absolutely no reason why a life dedicated to winning, whether in business, politics, sports or anything else, cannot also include the fulfilling pursuit of happiness through love.

In the first place, although dedication to your goal is a prerequisite of winning and nothing should be allowed to distract you from it, a love relationship of any sort is not a hindrance but a help: it provides motivation, it keeps you plugging away when you get discouraged, it gives you an incentive to overcome obstacles, and mainly it prevents you from becoming a lopsided person—a dehumanized success machine. *Love is such a vital, vibrant and positive force in the human equation that no amount of success can compensate for its loss.*

In the second place, earning and keeping someone's love is also a major part of any true winner's personality. To win, you must be able to relate to people, to influence and motivate them—in other words, to sell them on yourself. Quite naturally, this applies to intimate relations and social situations as well. As a rule *winners enjoy loving and being loved*; to ask them to give it up in the name of success would be to go against nature, and that's never a good idea.

Your decision to become a habitual winner should not hinder your romantic life. It may leave you a little less time for love, but it will enhance your pleasure. As a winner, you will be adopting a more optimistic, radiantly enthusiastic attitude toward everything you do, and it will carry over into your personal affairs. Love responds extremely well to positive energies, and you may find a depth of response you never before thought possible.

Just remember love's delicate, capricious nature and do not frighten it away. *Be the best person you can be, and love will come to you of its own accord.*

6. Marriage and family life

Notwithstanding temporary trends indicating its breakdown, the family as a social unit is still an essential ingredient of any really successful society. Collectivism, whether practiced by a commune or by a whole nation, as in Soviet Russia, has never produced anything remotely close to the living standard achieved by family-oriented social systems. Neither have societies based on casual attachments with no family responsibilities—an approach advocated in some quarters today—produced anything but a lot of neurotic, lonely people desperately seeking fellow "swingers."

For most winners, there is no more powerful motivation to succeed than family. Knowing that someone you love is behind you, supports you, rejoices in your triumphs and shares your home can inspire you to efforts you never thought you were capable of!

The process of acquiring a spouse and ensuring a happy and productive family life differs substantially from that of acquiring a business property. Anyone who tries to apply the same technique to both is sure to go down in defeat. As I said before, and as you no doubt learned during your adolescent skirmishes with love, you cannot bully, coerce or force someone to love you. Many otherwise successful people strike out in the love department because they are too impatient. In business and in your career, impatience can work wonders because it makes you want to win faster. In love, it is disastrous. Patience and persuasion are the proper techniques. You must give love a chance to germinate and come to full bloom at its own pace.

Sensual gratification, while part of this process, is only a by-product of love, and it has been badly oversold in our mass culture. As a result, many people marry without waiting to discover the person behind the sexual thrill. Once the fires of passion die, they find that they are left with just a person—the same man or woman they started out with, nothing more and nothing less. Their hour of madness is over, and they now face a dreary future of trying to rekindle the sexual spark—which of course is impossible. There are some things you cannot recapture, and only a fool keeps trying.

You can find happiness only if you start out with someone you enjoy, someone you like as a person. In this case, your relationship is not behind you but before you. True, you will no longer have a "lover." But if you're honest with yourself, and if you disregard the insane popular myth that everyone has to "score" all the time to be happy, then you will admit that you don't really want one anymore. What you want now is something much more demanding: a wife, a mother; a husband, a father; a companion, supporter and comforter.

To succeed in the game of love, you must understand its peculiar characteristics, which are quite the opposite of those that prevail in other competitive fields. Love is giving, not getting; it is the labor of love that provides joy, not the wages; the game counts, not the score. The lover's delight is to yield, not to claim. *Love is doing, not having.* After all, the mountain climber strives only to reach the peak, not to possess it.

It is the same with marriage. Fools marry thinking they will get something out of it—that is, as an act of self-indulgence. The wise man and woman know that the real rewards of marriage, its only lasting qualities, are toil, duty, responsibility; it is these that help you attain maturity—manhood, womanhood—in the fullest sense. You don't mature simply by aging: it's a matter of acquiring wisdom.

The successful marriage is an act of religious profundity—the sacrifice of Self on the altar of Family, the basic social unit that has been the key to the development of civilization and culture. Thus, you win only if your marriage is viable, and it is viable only if it produces something useful and enhances the lives of both partners—children, perhaps, or a home instead of what used to be only "a place to live." You prosper only if the unit prospers; you can be happy only if the whole family is happy.

Marriage is the ultimate partnership. As we have seen, partnerships almost never work in business, where you are limited to seeking a partner with suitable professional capabilities. You have neither the time nor the inclination to look for a compatible personality as well, yet the dissonant personalities of the partners have a way of clashing with melancholy regularity. In marriage, however, partnerships can work as long as the elusive quality called compatibility exists on every level.

In every healthy heterosexual relationship, the man plays a dominant role, the woman a passive one. This is natural, and no amount of propaganda by the rabid equalizers will change it. If you strive for parity, you'll get mediocrity every time. Accept the role nature assigned you; it's the only way to make the whole work. The fact that the man is dominant doesn't make the contribution of the woman any less *valuable*: the passive partner contributes just as much to the total as the active one. *That's* the true meaning of sexual equality.

Never marry a person you do not both love and respect. Love lasts for a while, respect forever. If you respect someone, then the little acts of courtesy, consideration, patience and understanding that form such a large and important part of everyday life will come naturally and will not have to be forced.

Do not take your mate for granted once you are married. In old-fashioned households, the stove had to be freshly lit every morning. Today our physical lives have become automated, but not our emotional lives. Hence, the spark of affection that keeps the marriage warm has to be rekindled daily, no matter how sophisticated we fondly imagine we have become. It actually takes very little to keep the flame going—a kind word, a smile, a token present, a little effort. But these gestures are more important than most people realize. *In love and marriage, small investments bear big dividends.*

When problems arise at work or at home, remember that the marriage unit is there to disperse pressure and distribute the load.

Don't take things out on your spouse—share them instead. Never waste time trying to put the blame where it belongs. Use time creatively by suggesting how things went wrong and can be put right. Do not criticize, belittle or put down. Those are negative approaches; you will almost always get better results, and without an aftertaste of rancor, by taking a positive approach. Don't say, "You look terrible in red" when you can say, "I think I'd like you even better in blue."

Love and marriage are social skills of paramount importance. True, anyone can experience love without premeditation, but that does not mean you can't increase your fulfillment and enhance your capacity for creative love by applying intelligence and common sense. Should you marry at all? I go with Socrates: "By all means, marry. If you have a good spouse, you will be very happy. If you have a bad one, you can become a philosopher."

Always remember that in love the art of winning is a different proposition. *In love, the winner is the one who can give the most.*

7. Winning in sports and games

Vince Lombardi, the coach of the Green Bay Packers, used to say, "Winning isn't everything—*it's the only thing!*" This is really a bit of sophistry: if you analyze it carefully, it doesn't mean much by the strict rules of logic. But it sparkles and gets the point across.

The point is that in order to win, you must lock your mind in a position where winning is the only thing in it. Given two opponents or two teams of equal ability, the one with a more positive mental attitude invariably wins.

When a survey compared team policies with results in pro football, it was discovered that contrary to expectations, the teams that spent the most time practicing were not the big winners. The teams whose coaches spent the most time instilling winning attitudes in their players were the ones that won the largest percentage of their games!

The winning attitude is a psychological factor with little tangible ground and almost no rational explanation. It is a fragile thing and must be nurtured very carefully. Note, for example, how much importance is attached in sports to such things as playing at home, the support of the fans, cheerleaders, good press relations and a harmonious atmosphere in the locker room. None of these appears to have much to do with the game itself, and yet everyone knows they affect the playing just the same.

And don't forget the opposite side of the coin, the fine art of psyching out the opposition. In 1561 Spanish bishop Ruy Lopez published one of the first books dealing with the game of chess. In it, he quite sincerely recommended placing the board so that the light shines in the opponent's eyes, blowing smoke in his face and making distracting noises and bodily movements. They may not have known much about sportsmanship in medieval times, but they most assuredly knew about the importance of putting the opponent on the defensive! Today we use much more sophisticated stratagems, but the basic idea is still the same: to distract the opponent, shake his faith in himself, insinuate into his mind the mere suggestion that he may lose.

The bottom line is that if you can sustain a firm belief in your own victory and at the same time erode the confidence of the opposition, the battle—whatever it is—is half won (assuming approximately equal ability and no intrusion of the element of chance).

How do you develop the winning attitude? Determine that you are there to win, and nothing else. Whatever the contest, *you* know that the only thing that matters is to win, And the only way to win is to beat the opponent fair and square. It will take one hundred percent of your effort, and you must be mentally ready to give it.

There is no one method of putting yourself into a winning frame of mind. You must find your own way. Successful athletes all have a favorite system for clearing the mind of everything irrelevant before a crucial event and concentrating all their energy on the task of winning. The soccer star Pélé always lay perfectly still, shielding his eyes, for about twenty-five minutes just before each game. Racing driver Jackie Stewart imagines his body inflating like a balloon until it fills the contours of the car; in this way he identifies himself physically with his machine. Football ace Tom Matte always takes his dog for a walk before a game; he claims that the pre-game tension in the locker room gets on his nerves, and so he avoids it until the last minute. In contrast, Muhammad Ali conducts a one-man show in his dressing room before a bout, boasting and joking, building up his ego and deflating the opponent's.

In the 1936 Olympics, Jesse Owens startled the world by winning every gold medal in sight, breaking records like so many matchsticks. Part of his inspiration derived from the fact that the games were held in Berlin, where Herr Hitler took every opportunity to praise the "Aryan race" and denigrate blacks. Owens had a burning desire to prove the stupidity of this racial attitude, and it helped him to turn in a magnificent performance that even he himself never again equaled. Conditions never again approached such an ideal "do-or-die" situation.

An even more potent force than pride or intense dislike is the noblest of human emotions, love. "Let's win one for the Gipper" has become a cliché, but it accurately points to the fact that most people will perform better if they are motivated by a desire to prove their love or devotion. It would be interesting to speculate how many millions of contests were won just because the participants wanted to show off for their loved ones. That's why many athletes recommend directing a few last-minute thoughts to a sweetheart, a parent or someone dear, someone to whom you want to "dedicate" your win.

Tennis pros Billie Jean King and Martina Navratilova get their adrenalin flowing by stomping their feet and insulting themselves whenever they make a mistake. They feel it makes them angry enough to want to win more than ever—and apparently it works for them. In a similar vein, other athletes focus on inanimate objects. A soccer goalie admits talking to the goal posts; others address hockey sticks or skis; pitchers often mumble to baseballs before going into the windup. Some golfers say they visualize a specific place on the green and try to "talk" the ball into going there. But whatever the technique, its aim is to concentrate energy and accomplish a specifically defined mission.

In every team sport, the player with the winning attitude stands out immediately; he or she is the one who always delivers a hundred-percent effort, who strives for the extra point, who covers for a teammate even if there seems to be no need. In a recent Olympic meet, one of the members of the American relay team sprained her ankle in training. Knowing she could probably do better than her substitute even with the injury, she said nothing, bandaged her foot as best she could, and next day ran her section of the race with all her might—although she collapsed in intense pain right afterwards.

When Hank Aaron connected with a ball one day, he knew he had a home run—and it was an important one, since it broke the record held for some forty years by Babe Ruth. Anyone would have forgiven him if he had just stood there and watched his masterpiece soar into the stands. But Aaron would never have been in a position to break Ruth's record if he had not developed in himself the discipline of a habitual winner. He didn't hesitate for a second; he dropped the bat and ran like hell around the bases—just in case it wasn't a homer after all and the ball remained in play. Unnecessary? It was that time, but this kind of extra exertion is what distinguishes a true winner from a person who sometimes wins.

During the Depression, Willie Mosconi, the billiards king, had a wife and family to support, and no job. His only income was from billiards. He could not let his family down; he was determined that they would suffer no deprivation. These thoughts made him work on his technique until he became a legend in his own time.

Of course, there are other athletes who claim that none of the psychological stuff works for them. Winning is its own best reward, they say. It's an ego trip, pure and simple. This viewpoint is at least as valid as any other. Who can say what makes a particular individual want to excel? You might as well claim it's magic.

Come to think of it, there is something mysterious and magic about winning. Certainly the payoff, in terms of the money or momentary fame, is almost never great enough to justify the exhilaration you feel when you've won a tough one. Perhaps winning is a basic human need that we do not fully understand. But who needs to? We can feel it, and that's what counts. Don't deny yourself the experience just because you cannot rationalize it!

Identify your game. Having trained your body, add your whole mind and soul. Use any motivation at all—or none, if that's your style. But *win, win, win!* To paraphrase another old chestnut, there may be better things and there may be worse things in this world—but *there is definitely nothing quite like winning!*

8. Winning in politics

Politics is the art of the possible. In order to win in politics, you must be the artful dodger, the great pretender, and the skillful compromiser all rolled into one. For some, politics holds a fascination that no other game can equal. For others, it is an arena they prefer to shun.

A friend of mine in public relations claims that he could get virtually anybody elected to any office, from dogcatcher to President of the United States, if only the candidate would agree to play strictly his way.

The campaign would saturate all media—posters, newspaper ads, TV spots—the works. There would be plenty of pictures of the candidate, always smiling, with the flag, with children, with pretty girls or with all of the above. He would be identified as "the choice of the people" and "the best man for the job." There would be rallies and parades, stirring music, cheerleaders, hotdogs and free beer. And that's all.

At no time would the candidate appear in person. His convictions, platform and position on issues would not be identified at all. The press would not be allowed to ask any questions about the candidate's beliefs and plans but could get any amount of information on his personal habits, marriage or romantic involvements, and business affairs.

My friend says, rather cynically, that with this technique he could get a rabid Ku Kluxer elected in an all-black district, and I'm not so sure he isn't right.

All of which is merely a colorful way of illustrating that getting elected, the first step to winning in politics, requires mastering the art of winning popularity contests.

Since the electorate is becoming more and more diversified, the successful politician must somehow convey the impression that he is deeply interested in a staggering variety of issues, many of which elicit diametrically opposite responses from various segments of his constituency. On a small scale, this is done by artfully dodging questions and uttering nothing but innocent platitudes. On a larger scale, such as in presidential campaigns, there has developed a whole scientific approach to the successful substitution of an *image* of the candidate for the real person. Many books have been written on this subject, so it would be fruitless to belabor the point.

Once your popularity and platitudes get you elected to office, other problems arise. You are now dealing with professional politicians, lobbyists representing a variety of special interests, pressure groups and sundry wheeler-dealers. You must accomplish the job you set out to do (whatever motivated you to get into politics in the first place) against this formidable array of persuaders, negotiators and influence peddlers.

And if it is your ambition to remain in politics, you are also faced with delivering on enough campaign promises to run for reelection or stand for a higher office. It's no secret that this often requires compromises and deals, payoffs and intrigues. You may find yourself lying down with some very strange bedfellows. Few other professions have a worse reputation for attracting a sizable contingent of rascals in addition to the honest and sincere idealists.

For all these reasons, winning in politics belongs to a rather special category. Basically, there are three entirely different breeds of politician, and to each "winning" means something else.

There are those who are interested purely in personal gain. Their aim is to get elected to an office where they will have enough power to fill many jobs with relatives and cronies, and then proceed to rip off the public. To these politicians, winning means siphoning off a maximum of public funds for private use.

Obviously, when such people win, everyone else loses; they are definitely not the kind of winners to admire or emulate.

At the other extreme are the completely idealistic politicians motivated by dedication to public service. Many such people start out with the idea of initiating a reform of some sort or proposing a specific piece of legislation. Once they get elected and find the existing power structure impenetrable, they either resign in disgust or more often stay on in the hope of influencing at least some decisions or helping to shift the balance of power.

These people are more to be pitied than censured. Their intentions are honorable, but their chances of success are poor. Once in a while, they may find themselves in a position to perform a good deed for the public; most of the time, however, they must be satisfied with making a few small ripples in the stagnant pool of politics. Despite their electoral victories, it is rather difficult to conceive of them as winners—unless you are willing to consider small, often insignificant gains achieved at the cost of much wasted time and effort a win. I have yet to meet a politician who could point to a clear-cut, uncompromised, undiluted win and claim it as his personal achievement.

In my hometown in Kentucky, shortly after World War II, returning veterans were a major political force, and a group of them decided to challenge the established local government, which they saw as corrupt. They ran on a reform ticket and swept the election. Within a few years, the professionals had things all to themselves again. The reformers found themselves stymied and compromised on every side. Their proposals met with doubt, their bills got tangled in subcommittees, and everything proceeded at a snail's pace. Some of them decided sensibly that no real satisfaction was possible in politics, and they went back to their original trades. Others decided they couldn't fight the system until they joined it and in time became indistinguishable from the fellows they had hoped to banish forever.

If you are a "man with a mission," I don't recommend politics as the way to become a winner in the full sense of the word. I don't entirely rule out success, but your practical chances of winning are remote. You would have to learn to accept as a win any progress toward your overall aim, however small. Only an elected dictator might hope to accomplish all he has set out to do in politics—but there is no such animal. (True, dictatorships sometimes enact periodic rituals called elections, but outside of the name they bear no resemblance to the political process we know.)

The only people who can honestly claim to be winners in politics are those who belong to the third category. Neither cynical crooks nor naive idealists, they are in the game because they enjoy playing it. They like community affairs, they like persuading others to accept their views, they like the give-and-take of the democratic process, they like the power, influence and popularity political life offers to its successful practitioners.

If you fall into this category—the pragmatic politician—you expect neither quick private gain nor perfect solutions to social problems. You can become a winner by carving out an outstanding career in a difficult, demanding field. You can elicit both respect from fellow politicians and confidence from your electorate—a genuine and worthy achievement.

To win in politics, you cannot think in absolutes. You must try to please most of the people most of the time, which virtually requires that you be a middle-of-the-roader. If you do have any radical or unorthodox opinions, keep them strictly to yourself; people do not vote for candidates who alarm them.

Although a pleasant personality and the ability to get along with many different types of people are important to all winners, a politician needs an extra dose of both qualities. His convictions, integrity and spinal fortitude will probably be more severely tested in politics than in most other fields of endeavor.

Since politics is basically manipulation of people, there is a generous sprinkling of power-hungry, unscrupulous individuals in it. As a result, comparatively few people of high moral standards take it up as a career; if you have moral fiber, you may find yourself lonesome. This is a national shame. If, after considering all the pros and cons, you are still challenged by the excitement of the political arena, by all means take the plunge. We could use a few honest political winners.

9. Leadership

It has been said that a leader has two traits that set him apart from the crowd: one, he is going somewhere, and two, he can take others with him. But we are speaking of winners. To be both a leader and a winner, you must have one more qualification: *you must be going in the right direction.* Without this proviso, the original definition—going somewhere and taking others along—is satisfied by Adolf Hitler or more recently by Jim Jones, who led people to mass suicide in Guyana.

Why is it that so many people seem willing to follow leaders who are harebrained or positively evil? The answer is basically threefold, and it is an irresistible package to the very simple mind on the one hand, and the very twisted mind on the other.

One, even a deranged leader offers an alternative to aimlessness. He is definitely going *somewhere,* and most people's lives are so drab and purposeless that *anything* appears preferable to inaction.

Two, the bad leader always offers glib, easy answers—panaceas that attract the lunatic fringe as well as the extremely naive who still live in a simple, clear-cut dream world. Thus, Hitler had only to say the whole answer lay in eliminating the Jews.

Three, the bad leader invariably relieves his followers of the one thing that seems to scare them most: responsibility for their actions. Note how many of the fanatic cults that attract the brainless require you to sign over all your property to the group and put your whole life in its care. There is no need to make decisions; you can live in a child's carefree world, with all decisions made for you by the leader.

Take a recent classic example. The whole nation wondered what Patty Hearst, a rich, well-educated kid, could have in common with a group of repugnant thugs called the Symbionese Liberation Army. How could she join them, tortured or not? The answer is simple. Her life was serene but aimless; they supplied an aim (to seize power). She worried about the complexity of life; they told her that robbing the rich would solve everything. She had trouble making up her mind what to do with herself; they solved her problem by giving her clear, direct orders. We may never know exactly how much persuasion or brainwashing it took to sell the old magic three-way package, but we do know that eventually its fatal pull worked again, as it always does on a gullible subject.

While this case proves that the dynamics of leadership are extremely potent, it also points out that bad leadership inevitably results in disaster. Therefore, to reiterate, if you have leadership qualities you must lead in the right direction to be a winner. The wrong-way leader may score a few temporary successes, but in the long run he is doomed.

As a leader for the right cause, you have two strikes against you: you must respect the truth, which means you can never offer easy answers; and you must respect people's rights, which means you can never take over their property, life and responsibilities. Your followers must make their own decisions. This means that you can safely offer only the first of the three functions mentioned above: the alternative to inaction. You must be going somewhere, and you must motivate others to do the same.

You can assume that people like being led. If you don't care who you lead or where, it's easy to become a leader. After all, every street gang has one. A little charisma is all it takes. But to be a leader *and* a winner, charisma is not enough. You must care where you're going and with whom: *you need character and integrity.*

You don't want to lead the fanatics and the loonies, and you don't want to be a messiah. All you want is success for yourself; if anyone wants to follow your lead and try a similar approach, it's their decision and you cannot object. This, in fact, is the best way to lead: by example, not by speeches; by reason, not by emotion; by encouragement, not by coercion. Just do the best you can for yourself, and that's leadership enough, the purest approach.

As noted elsewhere, there is also a pragmatic approach to leadership: find out where people are going anyway, and then get in front of the column and take them there. This requires a bit of sixth sense—you must be able to define trends before they become generally recognized as such—but it is of course the safest way.

Naturally, it's not easy. Detecting trends in every field has become a veritable industry. There are organizations of every type that do product testing, poll taking, market analysis and surveys, so that no major change in tastes remains unknown for very long. Thus, you must spot a trend before it shows up in the professionals' charts (or before they think of asking the questions that would reveal it), and then you must act before others do.

As the world becomes more organized, orderly and mass-directed, leadership is increasingly one of the qualities on the critical list. More and more people are finding life a drab treadmill and are ready to follow any leader who can give them a fresh sense of direction. If you can provide effective leadership in a positive cause, the world will be at your feet.

To be a leader, be a winner first. People like winners, are attracted to them, want to be like them. And by this subtle process, a winner becomes a leader.

10. Winning and motivation

Archimedes maintained that given a fixed point in space to use as a fulcrum, he could build a lever and move the earth from its orbit. Such a fulcrum does not actually exist, but a strong, win-oriented mind can serve the same function. A strong will in conjunction with such a mind can then act as the lever.

As we know, exceptional individuals who can motivate others have often literally moved the world. They have been able to transport masses of people from place to place, wage wars, create empires, eclipse existing civilizations and build new ones. They have founded religions, formulated philosophies, created nations, and remapped the world many times over. There is no doubt that those who can successfully motivate others virtually own the world.

But who motivates the motivators? The answer is that they are self-motivated—a rare quality. At least ninety-nine percent of people are what sociologists call other-directed; they run with the pack, they follow their leaders. Even people who lead and motivate others on a small scale need not be totally self-motivated.

A coach leads and motivates his players according to well-known and established techniques that anyone with a little incentive could learn. Factory foremen and department heads are leaders who motivate, but the science of management is so well explored that this kind of leadership can be exercised purely by formula. It's the individuals who blaze new trails and set new trends who use self-motivation. Where there is no manual to memorize, no precedent to follow—in other words, when you have dared to step off the beaten path—you have to supply your own motivation.

Where do the self-starters turn? It may be called God, philosophy, the power of positive thinking or the superego—and probably goes by many other names. Whatever it's called, some people can summon from deep within themselves a tremendous power that overcomes inertia, drives them on to success and makes them winners. Where is this power? Can anyone find it in himself? If your soul is in harmony with your mind, you have a good chance. If I sound a little mystical at this point, bear with me.

Let's oversimplify and begin by supposing that in order to be a winner, you must like yourself. You must be convinced beyond any shadow of a doubt that the gift of life you've been granted is the greatest thing in the world; that it is worthwhile to use it to your best possible advantage; that the body given to you is an eminently suitable vehicle for this enterprise and should be kept in shape for the purpose.

If this sounds easy, it isn't. The part of you that has to believe all this is the part of your subconscious that regulates your life *without your control.* And therein lies the snag.

Unfortunately, many people do not really like themselves much. They think they do, but their actions prove otherwise. Millions and millions of people spend most of their adult lives committing slow suicide. They fill their bodies with poisons they know to be harmful; they overindulge in physical pleasures and time-wasting indolence that slows them down; they stultify their minds with empty diversions so that they will never be able to realize a tenth of their potential.

Do you think the streetwalker really likes herself? If she did, why would she cheapen herself, offer her body like a hunk of meat and keep company with the lowest classes? Does the chain smoker, who with every cigarette invites cancer to gnaw his insides, really have any respect for himself? Does the criminal, who risks long years of imprisonment under the most humiliating, subhuman conditions, really want the best for himself?

These people are losers because somewhere in their psyches they hate their lives. They either feel unworthy of self-respect (since our subconscious knows *everything* about us, maybe they have their reasons) or unable to deal with the kind of existence thrust upon them. And so their minds decide secretly, on their own, to destroy this unsatisfactory life. Since most people are hesitant to take their lives by direct action, they follow the command of the subconscious mind in more gradual, subtle ways. But destroy themselves they do!

Remember Marilyn Monroe? She had fame, beauty, money, a career and the admiration of millions of fans. Yet she obviously had one person against her—herself. And so she destroyed herself. For reasons we can never know, she did not find the meaning every life must have if it is worth the effort to carry on with it. There lies the crux of the matter. You must find this meaning and believe in it, or else you cannot possibly give your best. Your subconscious mind will prevent you. You must discover for yourself why life is a great thing and why you should live it to the fullest. You must keenly feel that you want to unleash the potential locked within you, and that it is good and proper to use all your energies to make yourself a winner in everything you undertake. You must keep firmly in mind that getting the maximum benefit out of life (without, of course, hurting anyone else) is a desirable goal, and in the long run the very best possible course for yourself, your family, and also your country and all of humanity.

The famous pioneer spirit that made our nation so great at the beginning of its history was forged by nothing more than a collection of individuals who desired above all to be winners. Since there was a large percentage of winners, everyone benefited and general prosperity ensued. Today we have a very low percentage of winners in our society, and everyone is a loser for it. We have become known as a "can't-do" nation. We can't win wars; we can't resolve crises; we can't initiate action; we can't deal with energy shortages; we can't lick inflation; we can't clean up the environment. Not because we *really* can't, because we think we can't and therefore do not bother to try our best.

The same is true of individuals. If you think you're a nobody, have no faith in your abilities, feel your mind is too feeble to deal with life on a big scale—why, you've talked yourself right into staying a loser, brother! In order to get moving, you must believe that everything you're doing is for the greatest and most important person in the whole wide world—yourself. You certainly wouldn't put out your best effort for anyone less, would you?

How can you foster this belief and make it strong enough so that even your subconscious hears about it? *Stay in harmony with yourself.* You have instincts, whether you admit it or not; listen to them. Do what you feel is right, not what you're being pushed into against your will. Don't hush the inner voice that tells you what's right and what's wrong; obey it.

Find out what inspires you most and follow it. Love for another person may be the greatest inner motivation; the love of God often inspires the spiritually minded, and love of humanity is another powerful force. You must believe in the dignity and nobility of life and want to express it. Your purpose must be to take the existence you started with and bring it to a higher level. You must know that a better life is possible and that it can be realized here on earth by your own efforts. Then, and only then, will you be a true self-starter and a winner.

Consider yourself a noble cause, and your exertions on your own behalf will then be justified.

11. Winning and religion

Over the centuries, one of the most powerful motivating forces of history has been religious faith. It has moved people to transcend their limitations and accomplish incredible deeds. It has been one of the great educating and elevating influences of mankind, slowly raising it from a purely animalistic existence to a higher social order. The missionary who faced unknown dangers and hostile natives, the monk who lived in ascetic seclusion to teach and inspire others, the peasants who built enormous cathedrals, pyramids and temples—all were accomplishing things that seemed impossible given their limited talents and powers; and yet they were done.

Unfortunately, religion has always contained a potential for harm, as well. The Crusades, the Inquisition, the conflict between Church and State—all were the result of misdirected religious zeal. As different religions proliferated, each claimed superiority over the others, and its adherents were usually ready to prove it with anything from bludgeons to missiles. The history of religion can be summed up in an analogy with nuclear power: there is enormous potential for good here, but in tapping it we must be careful not to unleash the explosive force instead.

To make religion yield its inspirational powers without alienating you from the rest of the human race, you must use it wisely. First of all, it should be a private matter between you and your God; religion is not to be sold, advertised, worn like a badge or in any way imposed upon others. Religion should be a set of moral standards to live by, and nothing else. It should give you the moral and spiritual backbone you need to become a winner in life.

A faith that deviates from these guidelines and intrudes upon other aspects of your life is suspect. A faith that makes you give up your ordinary life and possessions and herds you off to seclusion somewhere is transgressing its spiritual boundaries; it is becoming a political regime, and that has always been a failure.

A faith that forces you to go out and convert others as the price of admission is definitely unworthy of your time; you might as well be selling magazine subscriptions. Common sense tells you that human dignity and the nobility of the soul cannot be peddled like apples.

A faith that tells you other religions are inferior or asks you to discriminate against them in any way (such as refusing to marry someone of another faith) is wrong. So is any faith that would have you resort to violence and war against people of different beliefs.

Again, this is just common sense. Anything on this planet that brings people together, reinforces our common bonds and makes us love one another must be good. By the same token, whatever tends to separate us or turn us against each other must be bad. You do not win arguments about God with insults, fists or guns. Tolerance of other people's *beliefs* must be total—provided that their beliefs do not sanction actions harmful to you.

To make religion work for you and help you be a winner, take your spiritual guidance from it but avoid the unnecessary burdens that have found their way into most religions over the centuries. Don't bother yourself with time-encrusted dogma. Religion should be a living, positive spirit, not a matter of whether the world was created in one day or a thousand years. Such immaterial puzzles are good for nothing but aimless mental exercise; they will not help you decide how to treat your neighbor or what to do with your talents. Ritual too often degenerates into meaningless gesture. You can follow the moral principles of your faith quite well without bowing three times a day in the direction of Mecca, or any other purely external manifestation inherited blindly from medieval times.

Does your faith decree that you cannot do some things on given days or at given times? Consider: if you stand on one of the earth's poles, you can arbitrarily decide what time of day or even what day it is, simply by turning in a different direction. Does the designation of times and days, then, have any universal meaning? Of course not. In fact, once we are able to inhabit other planets or live in space stations, such minor details become totally inapplicable.

So if you cannot keep a business appointment because of some ancient superstition, you are only hurting and inconveniencing yourself without doing anything constructive to uphold your religious beliefs. If you live right and do right by others, no external proof is necessary; and if you don't, no amount of gestures will help.

Your religious faith should be a source of inner strength and firm conviction of your worth as a human being. If you find yourself worrying about whether you have followed some ritual or other, then it cannot be the kind of faith that will give you any real support.

If you are religious, by all means take from religion all your spiritual guidance and direction, but winnow out superfluous matters. *To be a winner, always take the best from any source.* Anything that leads you sideways or backwards is not a religion but a fraud. *Any real faith leads you straight up!*

12. Winners and losers

Some people object to the pursuit of winning at all costs. For every winner there must be a loser, they claim, and they feel sorry for the loser. Sheer bunk!

First of all, in many fields of achievement, your win will make everyone else better off. Let's say your winning idea starts a new industry and hundreds of new jobs are created. Everyone is a winner! If you win someone's love, both of you are winners. And if you edged someone else out, you may have prevented a mismatch that would never have worked out anyway.

Even in sports and other pursuits where there must be a win and a loss, the loser often gains in the process. No matter how good you are at your specialty, you cannot win every time; and the losses teach you the valuable lesson that anytime you relax your vigilance, anytime you have the wrong attitude, anytime you're in less than peak form, you are sure to get trounced.

Nearly every major win is accomplished at the price of a hundred losses, and learning to be a good loser is an important part of maturing. We all have a latent sympathy for the underdog—not the loser who slinks away to brood, but the loser who comes back to take another crack. There is nothing more satisfying in sports than to see the loser get up, brush himself off and come back to defeat the favorite. In New York, there was probably more cheering in 1969 when the last-place Mets slugged their way to a World Series title than in all the years the Yankees were on top. From the Yankees, every New Yorker expects a win; from the perennial losers, victory came as a once-in-a-lifetime thrill that will always be remembered.

Losers have a function. They provide the counterbalance, they flavor the winner's pot. They will have other chances to try for a win; quite often, a humiliating loss is the making of an eventual winner. Let's not waste any pity on the losers; *all the winners of today are yesterday's losers, and just look at them now!*

13. What price winning?

Throughout this book I have been stressing that winning is everything. I never said, and I hope no one will take me to mean, that winning is everything at *any* price.

We all value freedom. Therefore we understand that one person's freedom is unlimited only to the extent that it does not abridge anyone else's freedom. By the same token, you cannot have a worthwhile and permanent win if you do it by preventing someone else from competing. Any use of coercion, violence, cheating, threats, bribes or other means of fixing the game in your favor automatically nullifies a win, whether you are caught or not.

You cannot enjoy a win if you make others pay for it. If your goals involve a team effort, make sure the team is composed of volunteers. Do not drain the resources of your family and friends to finance your win, unless such help is freely offered. And if others have helped to shoulder the burden while the going was tough, do not forget that they are entitled to share equally in the fruits of the victory.

When pushing for a win, do it with all your might. But don't overdo it. Don't push so hard that you leave no time for being human; the win will give you little pleasure if it loses you the love of your wife, alienates you from your children and breaks up your family.

Do not trifle with your health. A win at the cost of ruined nerves, ulcers or worse is really a loss. You can make it without that million a little longer, but without your health, you're defeated forever! It is part of the winner's skill to set a pace that can be maintained without risking a physical breakdown. The student who keeps abreast of the subject is always more successful, and much wiser, than the one who lets things slide all semester and then spends two frantic days and nights without sleep, cramming for the finals.

Just as you should not use drugs to fool your mind into believing. it's doing great, you should also stay away from chemical means of fooling your body. When you're tired, don't use benzedrine; find the time to take a nap. When you're tense, make an effort to relax instead of reaching for the tranquilizers. Drugs of all types are crutches that will eventually enslave you if you abuse them; your win won't be worth much if you reach it as a quivering, pill-popping wreck.

Winning still is everything—but you must play the game by the rules.

14. Onward to victory!

Now that you've come this far, it's time for a decision. Weigh the pros and cons and decide which course you will take.

Be honest with yourself. On the one hand, you have a somewhat routine but generally comfortable life. Eight hours a day, five days a week, you're doing something that may bore you at times, but it will feed you and clothe you and permit you to use the rest of the time as you see fit. All in all, it's not too bad—millions have done it before and are still doing it and consider themselves quite happy. You may be like that too, and it's nothing to be ashamed of.

If that's the case, just put this book aside and go on as before. Don't bother making a halfhearted attempt if your whole being doesn't quiver with impatience to change your life; a minor, spare-time effort won't do it. But if your imagination has been fired and you definitely feel you have the makings of a winner, it's time to start making a few commitments to yourself.

First of all, you must realize that what I'm offering you is a full-time proposition. You must prepare for and mentally accept a total dedication to a single purpose—that of making yourself a winner.

Remember all the things I've been discussing? Well, you will have to do every one of them! And that takes hard work and effort.

You will have to take stock of yourself and chart the course that offers you the best chance.

You will have to marshal all your abilities and know-how, and acquire more if you need to.

You will have to learn the rules of whatever game you have chosen and then play it for all it's worth.

You will have to become a self-starter and a self-motivator, always alert for opportunities, always ready to try something new and different, always confident in yourself.

You will have to abandon established routines and get out of the ruts you may be wallowing in comfortably. Forget about regular hours, regular social life, regular periods of rest, weekends and time in general.

You will have to clear your mind for action, concentrate on a single subject and then work as if you were possessed by demons. Learn how to overcome inertia and how to use momentum.

You will have to accept the proposition that WINNING IS EVERYTHING and back it up with your whole heart. Go for the win with the stubbornness of a Missouri mule. Treat all setbacks as nothing but stepping-stones to your success. Persist, persevere and stick it out.

You will have to discipline your body to be subordinate and subservient to your mind. Forget excessive indulgence of any kind; forget drugs and alcohol; just stay healthy and trim.

You will have to discipline your mind to concentrate its power in the direction you have chosen. Make your win a shining beacon on which all your energy concentrates while everything else pales to insignificance.

You will have to overcome the fear of the unknown we are all born with, abandon any little cozy security blanket you are clinging to, and be prepared to plunge, take risks and seize opportunities.

You will have to resign yourself to the fact that you will often be out there all alone, fighting the established order or the powers that be, with all the odds stacked against you. And even at such times, you must retain complete confidence in yourself.

You must learn to exult in public and lick your wounds in private. Always smile, lead, encourage, radiate optimism. Never brood, retreat, cry, complain, give up.

I'm asking a hell of a lot, right? You bet your boots I am. But I have not asked you, anywhere in this book, to do anything I have not done myself. In fact, I've been through the whole mill, and as you can plainly see, I consider myself much better off for the experience. In fact, I still practice every one of the virtues described herein, day in and day out, and I wouldn't have it any other way. Winning is, I'm afraid, quite habit-forming, and I confess I'm a lifelong addict.

I sincerely hope that you decide to join me. *There's always room at the top!*

Epilog: Questions and Answers

Having finished this book, you should now have all the tools you need to go out and start making a winner of yourself. You may still have a few questions, but let me see if I can anticipate some of them and answer them in advance:

Q: Mr. Feltner, I have read your book, and it has done nothing for me. How come?

A: I have never claimed that *everyone* can be motivated. In fact, it's a rare quality, and I don't expect more than one out of a hundred readers to really go out and start doing the things I recommend. But the few that do *will* wind up winners— I guarantee that!

Q: Why aren't you more specific in your guidelines? Why do you deal so much in generalities and basics?

A: First, because generalities have broad validity, whereas specifics vary from person to person; and second, because an intelligent reader who has the winning potential needs only a start. If you have to be taken by the hand and led to every station in life, you're not a winner and very likely never will be.

Q: Books on how to be successful are a dime a dozen. Why do you think yours is any different? It covers the same subject, doesn't it?

A: Not quite. Success is a relative term, but in general all you need for success is capability and proficiency. I take this one step higher. My book is about winning, which requires total commitment and excellence. They are in essence the same as the two requirements for success, but honed to a much sharper edge.

Q: I object to your title, *Winning Is Everything.* Don't you think it's an immoral concept?

A: Not at all. For the last two decades or so, we Americans have gone through a period of breast-beating and shouting *"Mea culpa!"* We're ashamed of our wealth, of our power, of being better off than other nations. But that's ridiculous. We have earned it all, often through bloodshed but mostly through hard work. We have nothing to be ashamed of, and it's time we started being proud and self-confident. It's time we went out and won a few. Israel has done in the twentieth century what we did in the eighteenth, and they are not ashamed of what they've gained; in fact, they're damn proud of it, and should be. Why are we always so apologetic? If my title shocked you, well and good. I hope it also made you start to think.

Q: All right, suppose I take your word for it, leave my secure little job, set out on my own to be a winner—and fall flat on my face?

A: You'll have my sympathy, but nothing else. I told you to expect some rough sledding on the way! At first, you may hate me, but if you have any backbone at all, I am willing to bet that your failure will be the making of you in the long run, and years later you will want to thank me. Much depends on how you take the shock. If you get up and take another shot, you'll make it. If you stay down and continue blaming me, you have the makings of a first-class loser.

Q: I am married, and my family depends on my earnings. How can I take the kind of risks you are talking about?

A: There are winning individuals and winning marriages. In a winning marriage, both partners radiate unity of purpose. All major decisions are joint decisions, and all risks, failures and victories are cheerfully shared. This actually makes it *easier* to go for the kind of all-out effort I'm talking about, not harder.

Q: Do you yourself apply every principle you describe? If so, do you always win?

A: Yes, I certainly do try to apply all the principles set forth in this book. I don't smoke or drink, I always look on the positive side of the issue, and I have an intense desire to win at all times. When I turn my attention to anything, I give it all the concentration I am capable of. But I don't always win—far from it! It's just that the times I *do* win are so much more frequent than what most people consider "normal" (whatever that may mean) that obviously it's not just a matter of luck.

Let me put it this way: a few days ago I closed a deal that earned me a bigger profit than my father has earned in his whole lifetime (and he is still actively working). This one win alone has been worth all the extra effort I always put into everything—yet this is not the first time (and I assure you not the last, either) that I have had such success. Wouldn't you agree that a few good wins like this one compensate me for a hundred minor skirmishes I lost?